b⚬⚬zy brunch

The Quintessential Guide to Daytime Drinking

Peter Joseph

Photographs by Salma Khalil

TAYLOR TRADE PUBLISHING

Lanham · New York · Boulder · Toronto · Plymouth, UK

Published by Taylor Trade Publishing
An imprint of The Rowman & Littlefield Publishing Group, Inc.
4501 Forbes Boulevard, Suite 200, Lanham, Maryland 20706
www.rowman.com

Estover Road, Plymouth PL6 7PY, United Kingdom

Distributed by National Book Network

British Library Cataloguing in Publication Information Available

Library of Congress Cataloging-in-Publication Data
Joseph, Peter
Boozy brunch : the quintessential guide to daytime drinking / Peter Joseph ; photographs by Salma Khalil.
p. cm.
Includes bibliographical references and index.
ISBN 978-1-58979-678-2 (hardback) — ISBN 978-1-58979-679-9 (electronic)
1. Cocktails. 2. Brunches. 3. Cookbooks. I. Title.
TX951.J77 2012
641.87'4—dc23
2011051913

 ^{TM}

Printed in China

for katy

contents

introduction

All happiness
depends on a
leisurely breakfast.

—John Gunther

Would you like a Mimosa or a Bloody Mary? Stop by most restaurants on a **Sunday morning** (or, let's be honest, afternoon), and those will likely be your only options.

If you're lucky, you might find a Bellini or an Irish Coffee. Perhaps the limited cocktail menu can be chalked up to the bartender being a bit hung over, but most restaurants' cocktail repertoires don't get interesting until after five o'clock.

This either/or menu wasn't always the rule. People have been enjoying a nip at dawn since the dawn of civilization. Five thousand years ago Egyptians could upon waking look forward to a toothpaste made of wine and pumice. More recently, the effort to start the day off with a bit of the strong stuff has been part of America's patriotic tradition since George Washington marinated his dentures each night in a glass of port. Then, in the early nineteenth century, the cocktail arrived. Historian David Wondrich writes in *Imbibe!* that the first recorded mention of one appears in 1803, and it was drunk at 11 a.m. For the first several decades of its existence, the cocktail remained a morning "antifogmatic." If the term for brunch didn't exist yet, the intentions for it did.

It wasn't until 1895 when the concept of brunch, a leisurely meal that could last for any number of hours between morning and afternoon, entered the English language, in Guy Beringer's "Brunch: A Plea":

Instead of England's early Sunday dinner, a postchurch ordeal of heavy meats and savory pies, why not a new meal, served around noon, that starts with tea or coffee, marmalade and other breakfast fixtures before moving along to the heavier fare? By eliminating the need to get up early on Sunday, brunch would make life brighter for Saturday-night carousers. It would promote human happiness in other ways as well. Brunch is cheerful, sociable and inciting. It is talk-compelling. It puts you in a good temper, it makes you satisfied with yourself and your fellow beings, it sweeps away the worries and cobwebs of the week.

Even the term "brunch," clearly a portmanteau of "breakfast" and "lunch," had drinking built into its DNA. "Lunch" is an abbreviation of "luncheon," a corruption of the Middle English "nuncheon." "Nuncheon"—itself a portmanteau of "noon" and "scheken"—literally means "noon drinking."

More explicitly, Beringer suggested drinking wine and beer with brunch, forever joining the meal with libations. Ever since it's been the stage for experimentation. "Freedom is written into the charter of this oddity among meals," wrote the *New York Times* restaurant critic William Grimes in 1998. Unfortunately, the widespread and deceptively attractive offer of "all-you-can-drink" brunch specials has pressed standardization and simplification upon the hungry, hungover masses. Bloody Marys, Mimosas, and other easily produced (and often, sadly, watered down) tall drinks have doused the creativity that used to be present at the early morning breakfast table.

With the current boom in cocktail innovation, those subpar drinks may be headed for a watery grave. And it's this author's goal to speed their descent. In this book, I've set out to give you a selection of classic morning cocktails as well as creative alternatives to the contemporary set of champagne-, coffee-, tea-, fruit-, or vegetable juice–based recipes. There is also a selection of hangover cures for those in need of some additional support.

There's no reason to settle for just a few kinds of drinks every time you want a restorative brunch after a night out. You should be able to recover just as easily from last night's revelry with a Corpse Reviver, a White Lady, or a Bloody Bull. In these pages you have your pick of more than a hundred eye-opening recipes (including, yes, an Eye-Opener) to try, if not all in one go. (While I'm sure you don't need to be reminded to drink responsibly, let's just get that warning out there in case your teenage nephew picks up this book.)

But let's begin at the beginning, with a few classic cocktails that were a regular part of our ancestors' diet. With the craze for classic cocktails continuing unabated, the brunch menu can easily follow suit. In places such as New Orleans, the sanctuary of so many cocktail traditions, it may never have ceased.

Here, then, is a selection of older recipes that should be **welcomed back** to the breakfast table.

absinthe suissesse

makes 1 drink

This recipe comes from Chris Hannah, the head bartender at French 75, the bar at Arnaud's Restaurant in New Orleans.

¾ oz anisette

¾ oz absinthe

½ oz white crème de menthe

¼ oz Orgeat Syrup (or Simple Syrup)

1 egg white

1½ oz half-and-half

3 drops orange-blossom water

Combine the ingredients in a cocktail shaker with ice, "shake feverishly,"
and strain into a chilled wineglass.

milk punch

makes 1 drink

New Orleans bartender Chris Hannah recommends trying the Milk
Punch alongside a plate of Eggs Hussarde (recipe on pp. 14–15)

½ tsp nutmeg, freshly grated
1 ½ oz bourbon or brandy
1 tsp vanilla extract
¼ oz Simple Syrup
2 oz half-and-half

In a cocktail shaker with ice, add half of the nutmeg and the
other ingredients. Shake and pour into a double old-fashioned glass.
Garnish with the remainder of the nutmeg.

eggs hussarde

serves 8

What better recipe to use than that of another New Orleans institution, Brennan's, for this classic brunch dish? If you aren't able to find Holland rusks—a dry, crisp bread—then replace with toasted English muffins. I've adapted Brennan's recipe here.

for the marchand de vin sauce

6 tbsp butter
½ cup onion, finely chopped
1½ tsp garlic, finely chopped
½ scallion, finely chopped
½ cup boiled ham, finely chopped
½ cup mushrooms, finely chopped
⅓ cup all-purpose flour
2 tbsp Worcestershire sauce
2 cups beef stock
½ cup red wine
1½ tsp thyme leaves
1 bay leaf
½ cup fresh parsley, finely chopped
salt and pepper to taste

for the eggs

2 cups white vinegar
8 eggs
2 tbsp butter
8 slices Canadian bacon
8 Holland rusks

for the hollandaise sauce

12 tbsp unsalted butter
3 egg yolks
2–3 tbsp lemon juice, freshly squeezed
salt and white pepper to taste

For the Marchand de Vin sauce, melt the butter in a saucepan. Sauté the onion, garlic, scallions, and ham for about 5 minutes. Add the mushrooms, reduce the heat to medium, and cook for about 2 more minutes. Then mix in the flour and continue cooking, while stirring, for another 4 minutes. Now add the Worcestershire, stock, wine, thyme, and bay leaf. Simmer for about an hour, stirring occasionally. Remove the bay leaf, and then add the parsley. Salt and pepper to taste.

For the eggs, in a pot, bring 1½ quarts of water and the vinegar to a boil and then add the eggs carefully so as not to break the yolks. Cook for 3 to 4 minutes, and then remove with a slotted spoon and place in a bowl of cold water.

Fry the bacon in a pan with butter until brown, about 5 minutes. Then place on a baking sheet in the oven, set to 200°F, to keep warm.

To make the hollandaise, begin by melting butter in a pan over low heat. In a large saucepan, before placing on a burner, whisk together the eggs, lemon juice, 1 tbsp water, and salt and pepper until the mixture looks pale yellow in color. Set the heat to medium-low, place the saucepan on the burner, and continue whisking as the sauce cooks, until the whisk leaves trails in the eggs, or about 5 minutes. Remove the pan from the stove and begin whisking in the butter 1 tbsp at a time.

Once the sauce is ready, reheat the eggs in a skillet of water for about a minute. Use a slotted spoon to place the eggs on towels to drain. Plate the Holland rusks, then top each with one slice bacon. Spoon Marchand de Vin sauce over the bacon. Top with one egg each, and then spoon Hollandaise sauce over them.

mint julep

makes 1 drink

The julep was long the province of the doctor, in the days when medical professionals knew a good placebo when they saw one. Patients would take it in the morning, and there are still some days when it's the only remedy that will do. The brandy in this recipe can be substituted with the more common bourbon.

Try this drink alongside bacon, eggs, and grits.

1 tbsp bar sugar

2½ tbsp water

5–6 mint sprigs

3 oz brandy

berries for garnish

dash Jamaican rum

Dissolve the sugar in the water, and then press three or four sprigs of mint into the syrup. Add the brandy, then top with crushed or shaved ice. Garnish with remaining sprigs and berries, add the rum, and sprinkle with a little more bar sugar. Insert straw and treat the complaint.

While the notion of drinking cocktails directly after breakfast may seem at first consideration an eminently unchristian practice, this has not always been the case.

—Lucius Beebe,
The Stork Club Bar Book

pink lady

makes 1 drink

A variation on a White Lady, the grenadine adds some sweetness to the gin.

Pair with a shrimp or crabmeat omelet.

⅓ oz grenadine
1 oz gin
1 egg white

Combine the ingredients in a shaker with ice, then strain into a chilled cocktail glass.

punch romaine

A 1950s recipe that has been brought back to the brunch menu at Arnaud's in New Orleans, recommended by bartender Chris Hannah.

1 oz white rum
2 oz sauvignon blanc
½ oz lime juice
½ oz Simple Syrup
nutmeg, freshly grated, for garnish

Combine the ingredients in a shaker with ice. Shake, strain into a chilled champagne flute, and garnish with grated nutmeg.

ramos gin fizz

makes 1 drink

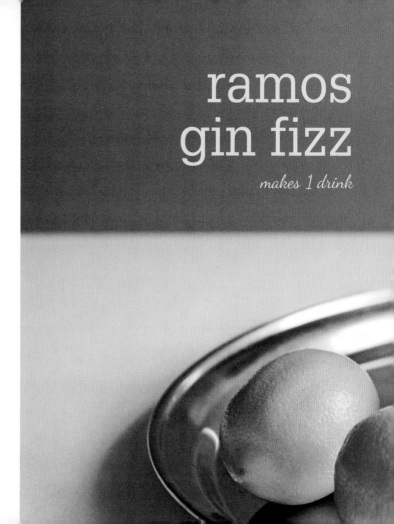

Invented by Henry C. Ramos in 1888, this drink was a favorite of Louisiana senator Huey Long, who flew a New Orleans bartender to New York to show Yankee bartenders how it was done.

2 oz London dry gin
1 oz heavy cream
1 egg white
½ oz lemon juice
½ oz lime juice
2 tsp bar sugar
2–3 drops orange-blossom water
club soda

Combine all but the soda in a shaker with ice, then shake for a minute or two (Ramos's bartender reportedly shook for 12 whole minutes). Pour into a chilled collins glass and top with soda.

sherry flip no. 1

A relatively low-alcohol choice for a brunch drink.

1 whole egg
1 tsp sugar
2 oz cream sherry
nutmeg, freshly grated, for garnish

Shake with ice and strain into a cocktail glass.
Top with nutmeg.

Woe unto them
that rise up
early in the morning,
that they may follow
strong drink.

—Isaiah

sherry flip no. 2

This recipe comes from Chicago's famed Pump Room, which opened in the late 1930s and played host to stars for decades.

1½ oz dry sherry

1 heaping tsp sugar

1 egg

3 dashes crème de cacao

2–3 dashes nutmeg, freshly grated,
    for garnish

Combine ingredients with a half cup of shaved ice in a blender and mix well. Pour into a chilled 5½-oz champagne glass. Top with nutmeg.

white lady

makes 1 drink

In its 1950s drink guide, *Esquire* recommends this cocktail to "soothe" your guests and suggests it be served for "business, visiting firemen, prospects, tycoons." This recipe comes to us via Academy Award–winning actress Judy Holliday. Perhaps this cocktail is what helped her avoid being blacklisted from films when she was questioned by the Senate Internal Security Subcommittee about her connections to communism.

3 or 4 oz gin

1 oz Cointreau

1 oz grapefruit juice, freshly squeezed

Combine in a shaker with ice, shake, and strain
into a chilled cocktail glass.

make your
coffee or tea
stronger

Only Irish coffee
provides
in a single glass
all four essential
food groups:
alcohol, caffeine,
sugar, and fat.

—Alex Levine

Coffee is itself a tried-and-true hangover cure, but it also has more scientifically sound benefits.

Current medical findings indicate that most us should drink a half-dozen cups a day if we're able to. (This excludes pregnant women, but if you're currently with child, congratulations! Now put this book down.) Coffee wards off health issues such as Parkinson's disease, heart disease, type 2 diabetes, cavities, colon cancer, prostate cancer, and perhaps most importantly for us drinkers, liver cirrhosis.

Tea has also been cited for its health benefits since early on in its adoption by the West. English diarist Samuel Pepys first tried tea in 1660, when it was just gaining steam in Britain. Within only seven years he was hearing claims of its curative powers. The antioxidants in tea actually make it better for you to drink than water, according to a study in the *European Journal of Clinical Nutrition* and as reported by the BBC in 2006. Also, the fluoride in tea can be good for your teeth.

Adding a little hair of the dog to your cup of tea or coffee will make for a much more interesting beverage to warm up to.

black rose

There are other drinks that claim this same name, but this recipe stands out.

Try with a breakfast pizza or a bacon, egg, and cheddar sandwich.

2 oz dark rum
1 tsp bar sugar
5 oz cold coffee

Combine the rum and sugar in a tumbler, stir to dissolve the sugar, add ice, and then fill with coffee.

The a.m. elbow bender is a Maverick, a lone wolf and there is no predicting his vagrant whim or fancy.

—Lucius Beebe,
The Stork Club Bar Book

blackjack

makes 1 drink

According to a 1940s *Esquire* article, it's a drink that
"will bring out the figure-skating-champ in you." While
I'm not quite sure what the author meant by that, it's a
worthy cocktail, one strong enough that after drinking it,
I might think twice before heading onto the ice.

This dry cocktail would go well with a sweet pastry
or even a chocolate-glazed donut or two.

¾ oz kirsch
1½ oz brandy
1½ oz cold coffee
lemon twist for garnish

In a cocktail shaker, combine the ingredients
with ice and shake. Strain into a cocktail glass.
Add garnish.

bradsell's vodka espresso

makes 1 drink

Created by London bartender Dick Bradsell when, legend has it, a model walked into his bar and asked him to make her something that would "wake me up, then fuck me up."

1½ oz vodka
¼ oz Simple Syrup
¾ oz Kahlúa
1 short espresso
3 coffee beans for garnish

Combine the ingredients, shake with ice, and strain into a chilled cocktail glass. Garnish with the beans. Can also be served on the rocks. Dale DeGroff suggests adding 1 oz of cream.

caffe vermouth

makes 1 drink

A sweet, milky drink with a low-alcohol and low-caffeine quotient. The vermouth goes surprisingly well with the coffee.

Try using a strong coffee—even espresso—in this recipe.

3 tbsp sweet vermouth
2 tbsp cold coffee
2 oz milk
1 tsp bar sugar
3 coffee beans for garnish

Combine ingredients in a shaker with ice. Strain into a cocktail glass and garnish with roasted coffee beans.

café brûlot diabolique

serves 4

This New Orleans classic calls for some unusual equipment, including a chafing dish or other metal bowl that can withstand a direct flame. Invented in the 1890s at Antoine's Restaurant in the French Quarter by the founder's son, Jules Alciatore, and possibly inspired by Brûlot Charentais, a similar French drink, the Café Brûlot is about showmanship as much as the ingredients. "When the famous Café Brûlot Diabolique is served at Antoine's, the lights are lowered in the restaurant," writes the Oscar-nominated author Mildred Cram in 1917's *Old Seaport Towns of the South*. "The serving of such a coffee becomes, appropriately, a rite, and it is a solemn moment when the silver bowls, ablaze with burning cognac, make their appearance in the crowded cafe. Strangely, since we claim to love freedom, it is ceremony and not license which appeals most strongly to our heart of hearts!" This observation might be applied to much of the cocktail craze.

2 sticks cinnamon

8 whole cloves

1 lemon peel

1½ tbsp sugar

3 oz brandy

3 cups strong hot coffee (preferably brewed using a French press)

In a heatproof bowl or chafing dish, combine the cinnamon, cloves, lemon peel, sugar, and brandy. Heat over an open flame without bringing to a boil, then ignite the brandy with a long match. Use a metal ladle to stir for two minutes. Add the coffee and dole out the mixture into demitasse cups.

Variations might use an orange-flavored liqueur such as Grand Marnier or curaçao and an orange peel instead of lemon.

cafe cocktail

makes 1 drink

Created by bartender Constantino Ribalaigua Vert at Cuba's El Floridita, the same man who shook up Ernest Hemingway's preferred style of daiquiri.

1 oz cognac
1 oz crème de cacao
2 oz coffee
1 tsp bar sugar
lemon twist for garnish

Combine cognac, crème de cacao, coffee, and sugar in a shaker filled with ice, stir, and strain into a cocktail glass. Garnish with the lemon twist.

café royale

makes 1 drink

The showstopper in bartending is, without a doubt, fire. The classic drink for this purpose is the Blue Blazer, which is simply Scotch and water tossed back and forth in a flaming arc between cups. Impressive, but not quite ideal for brunch. And perhaps you don't want to dim the lights and drag out the chafing dish required for a Café Brûlot Diabolique. The Café Royale is your single-serving recourse.

Try with beignets.

2 oz hot coffee
1 sugar cube
1½ oz brandy

Rest a spoon holding the sugar and brandy over a cup with the coffee. Set the brandy alight. Once the flame has died down, pour the brandy and sugar into the cup.

camel juice

makes 1 drink

An unusual combination of Galliano and Kahlúa.

Pair with a sweet brioche or other pastry.

1 oz Galliano

1 oz Kahlúa

1 oz brandy

¼ oz light rum

½ oz cold coffee

Combine the ingredients in a shaker with ice.

Shake and strain into a chilled cocktail glass.

coffee cocktail

I include this recipe for the name alone, though it lacks a key ingredient that you might expect in a Coffee Cocktail. The most obviously named cocktail in this chapter is guilty of false advertising. It also lacks the bitters that usually qualify a drink as a cocktail. "The name of this drink is a misnomer," writes Jerry Thomas in his bartending guide. "But it looks like coffee when it has been properly concocted, and hence probably its name."

1 oz brandy (Ted Haigh—a.k.a. Dr. Cocktail —recommends Martell)

1 egg

2–3 oz ruby port

1 tsp bar sugar

nutmeg, freshly grated

Add the brandy to your shaker, followed by the egg, then the port, and finally the sugar. Shake with ice and strain into a goblet. Grate a little nutmeg on top.

coffee frappé

The creator of this drink, George J. Kappeler, who was head bartender at Manhattan's Holland House Hotel, is also credited with the first published recipes for the Old Fashioned and the Widow's Kiss. So even this simple drink should be worth a try.

½ tsp bar sugar
2 oz cold coffee
1 oz brandy

Dissolve the sugar in the coffee and then add to a cocktail shaker along with the brandy and ice. Shake well and strain into a cocktail glass.

coffee granité

A homemade drink that might remind your guests of a frappuccino—only with an extra kick.

2 cups water
1 cup sugar
1 cup extra-strong espresso
4 oz coffee liqueur
heavy cream, whipped

Heat the water and dissolve the sugar in it, then add the espresso. Allow the mix to cool before pouring into ice-cube trays and keeping in the freezer until granular. Serve in stemmed glasses topped with the coffee liqueur and the whipped cream.

coffee nudge

makes 1 drink

Unless there's a bartender named Nudge out there, I expect this cocktail was named after its ability to nudge you awake.

Try with a plate of savory and sweet Chocolate Chip and Bacon Pancakes.

1 oz brandy
½ oz dark crème de cacao
½ oz coffee liqueur
5 oz hot coffee
Irish Coffee Whipped Cream
(recipe on p. 49)

In an Irish Coffee glass, build this drink and float the cream on top.

chocolate chip and bacon pancakes

serves 4 to 6

You could put almost anything in your pancakes, but after making these you probably won't want to try anything else. This recipe is J. Ross Marshall's adaptation of a *Cook's Illustrated* recipe.

5 slices bacon, cut into lardons
2 cups unbleached all-purpose flour
2 tbsp sugar
2 tsp baking powder
½ tsp baking soda
½ tsp table salt
1 egg
3 tbsp unsalted butter, melted and cooled
2 cups milk
2 tsp vegetable oil
½ cup chocolate chips
maple syrup and butter for serving

Cook the bacon lardons until crispy. Place on a paper towel and set aside.

In a medium bowl, whisk flour, sugar, baking powder, baking soda, and salt until combined. In a separate bowl, whisk the egg and melted butter into the milk until combined. In the bowl of flour and other ingredients, make a well in the center and pour in the milk mixture. Whisk gently until combined. It's okay for a few lumps to remain.

Heat a 12-inch nonstick skillet over medium heat, add 1 tsp oil, and coat the bottom of the skillet evenly. Pour ¼ cup batter onto three spots on skillet to form three 4-inch pancakes. Cook pancakes until large bubbles begin to appear, 1½ to 2 minutes. Add the bacon and chocolate chips to the uncooked side before flipping. Flip pancakes with a spatula and cook until golden brown on second side, another 1 to 1½ minutes. Repeat with remaining batter, using remaining vegetable oil only if necessary. Serve with butter and maple syrup.

39

coffee and rum

makes 1 drink

"For cold and sore throat," prescribes William "The Only William" Schmidt, bartender and author of the late-nineteenth-century cocktail guide *The Flowing Bowl*.

1 egg
1 tsp sugar
1 oz Jamaican rum
4 oz hot coffee
1 pat butter

Break the egg into a bowl and beat it.
Add the sugar and rum to it. Pour the mixture into a cup and add the coffee. Top with butter.

criterion coffee punch

makes 1 drink

This nineteenth-century drink from the American Bar of London's Criterion is credited to bartender (a.k.a. "well-known professor") Leo Engel. It is still served at the Criterion Restaurant today.

1 egg yolk
4 oz cold coffee
2 oz brandy
bar sugar to taste

Combine the ingredients and shake with ice and strain into a tumbler.

english cobbler

makes 1 drink

A variation on a classic drink, the Sherry Cobbler.

 Try pairing with the egg-in-toast
dish called Birds in a Nest.

1 oz lemon juice, freshly squeezed
1 tsp bar sugar
2 oz strong tea
4 oz Jamaican rum
berries for garnish (blackberries, raspberries)

In a highball glass with crushed ice, build the drink.
Garnish with the berries and serve with a straw.

green mar-tea-ni

makes 1 drink

From Marcia Simmons and Jonas Halpern's *DIY Cocktails*, this is a potent vodka cocktail with a hint of green tea.

1 ½ oz vodka
¾ oz Green Tea Syrup
¾ oz lemon juice

Combine your ingredients with ice in a cocktail shaker. Shake and strain into a chilled cocktail glass.

how to make green tea syrup

Vital for the Green Mar-tea-ni.

1 cup water
1 cup sugar
1 green tea bag

In a saucepan, bring the water and sugar to a boil before reducing the heat and adding the tea bag. Simmer for 5 minutes and then turn off heat before allowing the bag to steep for 10 minutes longer. Remove bag and store syrup in a jar or bottle in the fridge.

green tea punch

For a larger, more mature tea party.

16 oz hot green tea
9 oz red currant or guava jelly
4 oz brandy
4 oz light rum
2 oz curaçao
juice and peel of 2 lemons
verbena leaf for garnish

Combine the tea and jelly in a teapot, stirring until the jelly has dissolved. Afterward, add the rest of the ingredients and stir. Serve hot in mugs with a verbena leaf for garnish.

hot shot

makes 1 drink

An abbreviated coffee drink.

 Try alongside waffles topped
with a little more of the whipped cream.

½ oz Galliano
½ oz hot coffee
whipped cream

Add the Galliano and coffee to a shot glass,
and float the whipped cream on top.

irish coffee

makes 1 drink

"It's a bit of a pest to make, but never was such labor more richly rewarded," wrote Kingsley Amis. It was invented by chef Joe Sheridan, who first served it at the Foynes airport restaurant in Limerick in 1942 or 1943. Writer Stanton Delaplane sampled it there and then introduced it to the United States at San Francisco's Buena Vista Cafe a decade later.

2 oz Irish whiskey
5–6 oz hot coffee
2 tsp sugar (Sheridan used brown,
   but Buena Vista used cubes)
heavy cream, lightly whipped

Combine the whiskey, coffee, and sugar in a stemmed, heated glass mug and stir. Top with lightly whipped heavy cream. Pour the cream slowly over a spoon to create a clean layer above the coffee.

For a **Café Charentais**, substitute brandy for the Irish whiskey. For a **Café Jamaique**, use Jaimacan rum instead—or for a **Jamaican Coffee**, use less rum and also include Tia Maria. For a **Café Floride**, use an orange peel soaked in orange liqueur in place of the spirit. For a **Café Amore**, use amaretto and brandy. A **Calypso Coffee** calls for light rum and Kahlúa. **Mexican Coffee** calls for tequila and Kahlúa, while **Spanish Coffee** calls for Spanish brandy and Kahlúa, and a **Kioke Coffee** uses any other brandy and Kahlúa. A **Royale** requires cognac and sugar. And for the **President's Coffee**, use cherry brandy and add 1 tsp of grenadine to color the whipped cream.

james beard's irish coffee

makes 1 drink

Famed chef and food writer James Beard created this summertime option for die-hard fans of Irish Coffee.

 In hot weather, this goes well with a fruit salad.

1 cup hot coffee
¼ cup heavy cream
1 tsp bar sugar
2 tbsp Irish Coffee Whipped Cream
2 oz Irish whiskey
nutmeg or cinnamon for garnish

Combine the coffee, cream, and sugar, stirring to dissolve the sugar. Chill the mixture. Add 1 tbsp of whipped cream to a 14-oz highball glass, fill with the mixture, and then add three ice cubes and the whiskey. Top it off with the remaining whipped cream and a grate of nutmeg or cinnamon.

make
your own
irish coffee
whipped cream

makes 1 pint

1 pint heavy whipping cream
1 or 2 tbsp sugar (optional)
2 or 3 drops vanilla extract
(optional)

Take 1 pint of heavy whipping cream and pour into a steel pitcher or bowl (you can chill this container beforehand to speed up the process). Whisk until the air bubbles have disappeared but the cream isn't stiff. If you'd like it sweetened, add sugar to taste, 1 tbsp at a time, as well as 2 or 3 drops vanilla extract.

kilrain fight

makes 1 drink

Named after the 1899 bare-knuckle boxing match between John L. Sullivan and Jake Kilrain, this is probably the most breakfast-y drink in this book. Created by Derek Brown of DC's The Passenger, it has cereal in the mix.

1½ oz Irish whiskey (use John L. Sullivan 12-year if you can)
½ oz Cocoa-Infused Tea
½ oz Orgeat Syrup
½ oz lemon juice, freshly squeezed
mint sprig for garnish

For the Cocoa-Infused Tea

Crush a half cup of Cocoa Puffs and add to a pot of steeped black tea. Allow to sit overnight before straining through a fine sieve or cheesecloth.

Combine all ingredients except for the garnish with ice in a shaker. Shake until cold, strain into a chilled cocktail glass, and garnish with the mint sprig.

51

negrita

Suitably for a drink with espresso, this one comes as a shooter.

½ oz brandy
½ oz coffee liqueur
½ oz cold espresso

Combine all three ingredients in a shot glass.

negrita grog

Unlike the Negrita, this drink uses tea instead of coffee.

 Have a mug with a plate of banana pancakes.

1 oz brandy
1 oz light rum
1 tsp sugar
1 oz hot tea
1 tsp curaçao
lemon peel for garnish

Combine ingredients and pour into a large, heat-resistant glass. Fill rest of the glass with hot water and garnish with lemon peel.

nicoloscar

makes 1 drink

This barely qualifies as a shot, much less a drink. Still, if you're so eager for caffeine that you can't even wait long enough to boil water, then this is your answer.

1 slice lemon, trimmed of its peel
coarse-ground coffee
sugar
1½ oz brandy

Coat the lemon slice with the coffee and sugar. Chew the slice and wash it down with the brandy.

skier's
smoothie

makes 1 drink

Don't skip this because you dislike Galliano. If you've only had the Italian liqueur in Harvey Wallbangers and been left unimpressed, you'll be surprised by this recipe. The tea seems to transform the liqueur's flavors into something entirely different.

Serve with croissants or other pastries.

1½ oz Galliano
4½ oz hot tea

In a cup add the Galliano, then the tea.

vodka espresso

makes 1 drink

If you're looking for a cream liqueur other than Bailey's, then try Amarula, a South African variety.

2 tsp bar sugar
2 oz cool espresso or strong coffee
1 oz vodka
1 oz Amarula

Combine sugar, coffee, and vodka in a shaker with ice. Shake and strain into a cocktail glass. Add the float of Amarula.

more than
mimosas

Pleasure
without
champagne
is
purely
artificial.

—Oscar Wilde

Long before the Mimosa came into existence, poets praised the effects of a good Champagne Cocktail in the morning.

But the Mimosa's immediate predecessor, the Buck's Fizz, paved the way for the star of the breakfast table. Created by Malachy "Pat" McGarry of the Buck's Club in London, the Buck's Fizz was first recorded being served in 1921. A few years later, the Ritz in Paris debuted the Mimosa, a strikingly similar drink. The Mimosa won out over the Buck's Fizz in the end. Perhaps doubling the amount of champagne had something to do with it.

Champagne works well in any number of morning cocktails—and there's no need to stick with just orange juice—but for those who can't stand the bubbles, there are plenty of fruit juice–based drinks for those in need of vitamin C. In this chapter, you'll find options such as the Harvey Wallbanger and the Salty Dog. And for the frugal among us, there's always the White Trash Mimosa.

I first met this stunt drink at an early (well, noon) New Year's Day brunch, alongside the Egg and Cheese Strata (see p. 62). All you need is a packet of orange-flavored Emergen-C vitamin supplement mix and a Miller High Life, a.k.a. "the champagne of beers." Add the powder to the bottle of beer and voilà, a White Trash Mimosa.

It's not quite at the level of the cocktails that follow in this chapter, but it's a good reminder that if you're ever in a bind, without fresh juice or a decent bottle of champagne, there's always a way to enjoy yourself.

american flyer

makes 1 drink

Unless it was named after the American Flyer model train, this
drink serves as a suitable toast to the Wright brothers.

3 oz white rum
1 tbsp lime juice
½ tsp Simple Syrup
champagne or sparkling wine

Combine the rum, juice, and syrup in a shaker with ice.
Shake and strain into a chilled wine glass. Fill the remainder of the
glass with the champagne or sparkling wine.

bahia
breeze

makes 1 drink

Imagine how surprised the thousands of "vodka and cranberry" drinkers might be if they knew that they were ordering an actual cocktail. If only they called it by its proper name, the Cape Codder. But you didn't pick up this book to find out that vodka and cranberry go nicely together in a glass with ice. There are several options for transforming the simple Cape Codder into something new, the Bahia Breeze being one of them. Just as a Harvey Wallbanger raises a Screwdriver from rail drink déclassé, the Bahia Breeze lifts up the old combination of vodka and cranberry from the barroom floor.

Try pairing these long, fruity drinks with a savory dish such as the Egg and Cheese Strata (recipe on p. 62).

1½ oz gold tequila
4 oz pineapple juice
1½ oz cranberry juice
lime wedge for garnish

In a highball or double rocks glass, build this drink over ice in the order in which the ingredients are presented above.
Add the lime garnish.

egg and cheese strata

serves 6

This is a favorite brunch recipe because it's just so easy. I've served it on more than one New Year's Day morning, when after an evening of champagne you know the last thing you need is a lot of clanging around in the kitchen. Most strata recipes will tell you to place the ingredients in a baking or casserole dish. But this one gives a simple recipe a nicer presentation.

1 loaf French bread or other long loaf

3 tsp lemon juice

1 tsp olive oil

6 eggs

1 cup milk

1 cup parmesan cheese, grated

2 tbsp basil, chopped

salt and pepper to taste

Preheat the oven to 375°F.

Cut out the center of the loaf as if you're carving a canoe. Cut the removed bread into cubes and set aside. Baste the loaf with 2 tsp lemon juice and 1 tsp olive oil.

In a bowl, combine the eggs, milk, cheese, 1 tsp lemon juice, basil, salt, and pepper. Toss the bread cubes in the mix. Then pour the combination into the hollowed-out loaf.

Bake for another 30 minutes or until the top of the egg and cheese mixture is golden. Serve in slices.

bellini

makes 1 drink

"The thing about a bellini," says the titular character in Geoff Dyer's *Jeff in Venice, Death in Varanasi*, "is that it's actually an extremely refreshing drink." Even if his often came with a side of cocaine, Jeff wasn't wrong in the least. One of the most popular Mimosa variations, this cocktail got its start in 1948 at Harry's Bar in Venice, owned by Giuseppe Cipriani. Its color reminded him of the toga in a painting by the artist Giovanni Bellini, and thus the drink's name. As the Cipriani restaurant empire spread worldwide, so did its popular drink.

Have a glass with a serving of Eggs Florentine.

2 oz white peach puree
3½ oz prosecco or other dry
   sparkling wine

Start with the peach puree in the bottom of your mixing glass or shaker, no ice. Add the prosecco while pulling the puree up the side of the glass to combine them. Do this all slowly and gently so as not to flatten your prosecco. Strain into a champagne flute.

bitter french

makes 1 drink

A variation on the French 75 by Philip Ward of New York City's Mayahuel.

I'd suggest trying this somewhat dry, sparkling drink with the Niçoise Salad Sandwich.

1 oz gin
½ oz lemon juice
½ oz Simple Syrup
¼ oz Campari
2 oz champagne
grapefruit twist

Combine the first four ingredients in a shaker with ice, shake, and strain into a chilled champagne flute. Top with the champagne. Express the zest of the grapefruit over the top of the glass and discard the twist before serving.

niçoise salad sandwich *serves 2*

The Niçoise salad barely makes the effort to be a salad in the usual sense with its ingredients often arriving separated on the plate. This sandwich, adapted from a *Gourmet* magazine recipe, draws all the elements together for an easier way to enjoy all the flavors at once.

for the filling

½ of a small red onion, finely chopped
2 tbsp extra virgin olive oil,
    plus more for drizzling
1 tbsp red wine vinegar, plus more to taste
¼ tsp salt, plus more to taste
black pepper to taste
15-oz can tuna packed in olive oil
juice of ¼ lemon to taste

for the sandwich

2 ciabatta rolls
lettuce leaves
4 tomato slices
2–3 hard-boiled eggs
4 anchovy fillets, drained
8 Niçoise olives, pitted and sliced
1 scallion, chopped
1 radish, sliced

For the filling, combine the onions, oil, vinegar, salt, and pepper in a bowl. With your hands, mix and squeeze these ingredients for about 5 minutes. Then add the tuna, including the oil, and mix. Add lemon juice and more salt, pepper, or vinegar to taste.

For the sandwich, cut the rolls in half and place lettuce leaves on the bottom halves, followed by tomato slices. Then add the filling. Top with four slices of hard-boiled egg, two anchovy fillets, olives, scallions, and radishes. Drizzle with olive oil, and then cover with the top half of the roll.

black velvet

makes 1 drink

If you please. This drink was created at London's Brooks's Club in 1861 in honor of the death of Queen Victoria's husband, Prince Albert. Suitably for a funeral, it's a large drink.

 But if you're still hungry, then accompany this with a full English breakfast.

4 oz Guinness stout
4 oz champagne

Slowly pour the stout followed by the champagne into a collins glass and stir gently.

blue lagoon

makes 1 drink

The island of Curaçao ships only six hundred cases of authentic blue curaçao to the United States each year, though you can find many pretenders to the name—essentially colored orange curaçao—to make this drink.

○ ◯ Drink this with a cheeseburger,
maybe with an egg and sautéed onions on top.

¾ oz white rum
¾ oz dark rum
½ oz blue curaçao
3 oz orange juice
3 oz pineapple juice
dash Angostura bitters
pineapple slice or other fruit for garnish

Add all the ingredients to a shaker, along with ice.
Shake and strain into a large goblet filled with fresh ice. Add garnish.

Three be the
things I shall
never attain:
envy, content
and sufficient
champagne.

—Dorothy Parker

bob hope's rye lemonade

makes 1 drink

Hope was not known for drinking. So in the Bing Crosby and Bob Hope vehicle *Utopia*, when Hope orders a soft drink in a bar, he hides behind a bit of machismo. "Lemonade," he says. "In a dirty glass."

bar sugar for rimming
2 oz rye whiskey
4 oz fresh lemonade

Chill an old-fashioned glass and frost the rim with bar sugar. Fill with whiskey, lemonade, and ice.

breakfast martini

makes 1 drink

Created by Salvatore "The Maestro" Calabrese while he ran the bar at the Lanesborough Hotel in London. This may be his most well-known drink.

1½ oz gin
¾ oz Cointreau
¾ oz lemon juice, freshly squeezed
1 tsp medium-slice (not too much rind) marmalade
2 orange twists

Combine the ingredients (except the orange twists) in a shaker with ice and shake. Strain into a chilled cocktail glass and squeeze in one orange twist for flavor before discarding it. Garnish with the second twist.

buck's fizz

makes 1 drink

The classic, while similar to the Mimosa, tips the scales in favor of the juice. Some recipes call for floating grenadine on top. Reserve that trick for the sweet toothed and keep it simple with just OJ.

4 oz orange juice
2 oz champagne

In a champagne glass, pour the orange juice followed by the champagne.

caribbean whippet

makes 1 drink

This variation on a Greyhound can be made only with Ting, a grapefruit-flavored soda. You can find bottles of this Jamaican beverage in groceries that offer ethnic foods or online.

1 ½ oz vodka

Ting soda

In a collins glass over ice, build the drink in the order given above.

champagne cocktail

makes 1 drink

A truly classic cocktail, which was drunk as early as 1850 and considered a morning drink almost right away. That early iteration skipped the brandy, and you may as well, depending on the way your morning looks.

Switch the brandy with
a calvados for a **Cavalier Cocktail**.

1 sugar cube
2–3 dashes Angostura bitters
1½ oz brandy
champagne

Soak the sugar cube in bitters and place
at the bottom of a champagne glass. First pour
in the brandy, add the champagne, and add
an ice cube if you wish.

71

three champagne punches

At some point you'll want to be able to make everyone's drink at once and get back into the fray of the party. To aid you with that effort, here are three variations on champagne punch to serve you and your friends.

james beard version
makes 40 glasses

½ cup sugar
½ cup lemon juice (or juice of 2 lemons)
2 cups orange juice (or juice of 6 oranges)
2 750-ml bottles cognac
16 oz Cointreau
4 750-ml bottles champagne (or other sparkling wine)
grated zest of 4 lemons
20 thin slices of cucumber

In a large punch bowl, dissolve the sugar in the juice, and then add the cognac, Cointreau, champagne, and zest. Gently stir it all, and then add the cucumber slices as garnish. Keep cool on a bed of ice.

dale degroff
version *serves 10*

1 whole ripe pineapple,
   peeled and cubed

3 sweet oranges, peeled and chopped

2 sweet grapefruits, peeled and chopped

1 cup cherries, pitted (fresh or frozen)

½ cup pomegranate,
   separated from husk

½ cup sugar

12 oz maraschino liqueur

24 oz VS cognac

champagne

orange peel and fresh fruit for garnish

Muddle the fruit and sugar in a large bowl until you've dissolved the sugar. Pour the liqueur and cognac over the fruit, then cover the bowl in your fridge and let sit. After several hours, remove and stir the mixture. Strain and press the fruit to get all the liquid into a pitcher. Garnish the pitcher with the orange peel. Pour 2 oz of this mix into a wineglass with a few ice cubes. Top with champagne, and garnish the glass with fruit.

david wondrich version

1 bottle brut champagne
1 ½ oz brandy
1 ½ oz Cointreau
1 bottle club soda
1 orange rind
slices of pineapple
slices of oranges
mint
strawberries

Make a single large block of ice ahead of time. Place it in a punch bowl and add the liquid ingredients. Garnish with the fruit slices and mint, and crush the strawberries into the punch for added flavor.

I never
drink anything
stronger than
gin before
breakfast.

—W. C. Fields

death in the afternoon

Probably Ernest Hemingway's most famous nonliterary creation.

1 ½ oz pastis
champagne

In a chilled champagne glass, pour the pastis. Fill with champagne.

flirtini

This drink may be irrevocably associated with *Sex and the City*. Some fans of the cocktail hope to change that. Heavy metal drummer Richard Christy favors it but prefers to call it a "Viking Testicle."

2 pineapple cubes
½ oz Cointreau or triple sec
½ oz vodka
1 oz pineapple juice
3 oz champagne
cherry for garnish

Muddle your pineapple in a mixing glass, and then add the Cointreau, vodka, and juice. Stir with ice and strain into a chilled cocktail glass. Top with champagne and garnish with the cherry.

french 75

makes 1 drink

While it's often thought of as an evening drink, bartender Chris Hannah of New Orleans's French 75 bar discovered otherwise. "During Mardi Gras I had to work a couple mornings and the natural light, which I'm not used to, made this drink look like it was possessed when I was serving it. I even asked my coworkers what they thought of the French 75 in the day."

Hannah recommends trying it
with a poached egg dish.

2 tsp bar sugar
1 oz lemon juice
2 oz gin
champagne
lemon twist for garnish

In a highball glass, dissolve the sugar with the lemon juice and then add the gin,
followed by ice cubes and the champagne. Add garnish.

greyhound

makes 1 drink

A standard juice-and-vodka drink for those moments when you want grapefruit but don't want to try to wrestle with half of one.

Have a glass alongside a few slices of French toast.

2 oz vodka
5 oz grapefruit juice

In a collins glass with ice, build the drink.

harvey wallbanger

makes 1 drink

The only drink whose name is more well liked than its taste, this cocktail has survived simply because of the memorable, Pynchonian nature of its moniker. The truth, however, is a little more disappointing. If you don't care for the herbaceous bitterness of Galliano, try a Tequila Sunrise (p. 96).

Switch the vodka with tequila for a **Freddie Fudpucker**.

3 oz vodka
8 oz orange juice
2 tsp Galliano
cherry and orange slice for garnish

Fill a highball glass halfway with ice, and then pour the vodka and orange juice over the cubes. Float the Galliano over the top and add the garnish.

kir royale

makes 1 drink

Invented by Felix Kir, who became mayor of Dijon, France, following the end of World War II.

Try with a croque-madame.

½ oz crème de cassis
champagne

Add the cassis as a float to a nearly full glass of champagne.

lady germain

makes 1 drink

Created by bartender Chris Hannah.

1 sugar cube
1 strawberry
¼ oz lemon juice
1 oz London dry gin
½ oz St-Germain liqueur
2 oz champagne
lemon twist for garnish

Muddle the sugar cube with the strawberry and lemon juice in a cocktail shaker. Add the gin, St-Germain, and ice, and then shake. Strain into a chilled champagne flute and top with the champagne. Finish with the garnish.

le perroquet

makes 1 drink

An interesting mix of bitter and sweet flavors.

Pair this drink with a Niçoise or Caesar salad.

dash Campari
dash gin
2 oz orange juice
4 oz champagne
lemon twist
orange twist

In a champagne flute, pour the Campari, gin,
and orange juice before adding the champagne.
Garnish with the twists.

madras

makes 1 drink

The love child of a Screwdriver and a Cape Codder.

1½ oz vodka
4 oz orange juice
1½ oz cranberry juice
orange slice for garnish

In an ice-filled highball glass, build the drink
and add the garnish.

mimosa

makes 1 drink

The classic, from the Paris Ritz Hotel, circa 1925.

2 oz orange juice
4 oz champagne

In a champagne flute with a piece of ice, pour
the orange juice followed by the champagne.
Stir and serve.

I am easily
satisfied
with
the best.

—Winston Churchill,
on champagne

monferrato

makes 1 drink

Created by Leo Robitschek, previously head bartender of
Eleven Madison and now bar manager of NoMad NYC.

1 oz Cocchi Americano
½ oz Cointreau
3 dashes Peychaud's bitters
3 dashes Angostura bitters
4 oz brut champagne
orange twist

Build all ingredients except the champagne
and orange in a champagne flute. Top with
champagne, and express and add orange twist
to the glass.

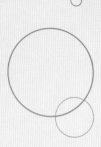

sparkling fluency

When you're picking out the right bottle for your champagne cocktails here are some terms that will help you make the right choice.

brut

The most common and what you ideally will want for your cocktail.

demi-sec and doux

Too sweet for most cocktails; save these for dessert.

extra dry

Sweeter than brut, but still can be used in cocktails.

sec

Sweeter than extra dry or brut, so not ideal for cocktails unless you have quite a sweet tooth.

traditional method, method traditionale, and méthode champenoise

Signifies that the bubbles were created naturally rather than artificially, which happens in some low-end lines.

morning glory

makes 1 drink

Said to have been created by the opera star Risë Stevens.

½ oz Cointreau
½ oz cherry brandy
dash Angostura bitters
1 each orange and pineapple slices
champagne

In a highball glass half-filled with ice, add the Cointreau, cherry brandy, and bitters.
Add fruit, and fill the rest of the glass with champagne.

papa's twinkle

makes 1 drink

This champagne-spiked interpretation of a Hemingway daiquiri may seem about as manly as Jake Barnes in *The Sun Also Rises* but is worth spending some time with.

½ oz light rum

1 oz grapefruit juice

¼ oz lime juice

¼ oz maraschino liqueur

¼ oz Simple Syrup

3 oz champagne

grapefruit piece for garnish

Shake the rum, juices, liqueur, and syrup in a cocktail shaker with ice. Strain into a flute or champagne glass, and top with the champagne. Garnish with a piece of grapefruit.

pineapple champagne cocktail

serves 6 to 8

This recipe is adapted from one served at Hollywood's Embassy Club. Opened by restaurateur Eddie Brandstatter in 1930 to give his film-star friends more breathing room than the touristy Cafe Montmartre next door, it had a limited membership of three hundred, which included boldface names like Charlie Chaplin and Gloria Swanson. You can still see Chaplin if you stop by today—the building now houses the Hollywood Wax Museum.

1 cup pineapple cubes

1 cup cherries

12 oz maraschino liqueur

2 oz lemon juice, freshly squeezed

1 750-ml bottle dry champagne

6–8 lemon peels for garnish

Place the fruit in a bowl and bruise it before adding the liqueur and juice. Marinate overnight in the refrigerator. Strain the marinade into a pitcher or bottle. In a chilled cocktail glass, add 2 oz of the marinade and top with champagne. Flame a lemon peel as garnish (see p. 91).

red hook criterium

makes 1 drink

Created by St. John Frizell, owner of Brooklyn's Fort Defiance, this drink is named in honor of a bicycle race that takes place in the middle of the night in the Red Hook neighborhood where the bar is located. The wee-hours annual race has also taken hold in Milan, where the amaro Rabarbaro Zucca hails from.

Frizell suggests pairing this drink with a plate of blood sausage, fried eggs, and toast.

1½ oz Rabarbaro Zucca amaro
1½ oz grapefruit juice
½ oz lemon juice
½ oz Simple Syrup
½ oz gin
club soda
grapefruit twist for garnish

Combine the amaro, juices, syrup, and gin in a shaker with ice. Shake and strain into a highball glass filled with ice. Top with soda, and garnish with a grapefruit twist.

the simple recipe for simple syrup

makes 4 cups

Simple syrup doesn't take long to make and offers an escape route for those of us who don't wish to dissolve sugar for one drink at a time.

Double the amount of sugar for **Rich Simple Syrup**.

4 cups or 1 part sugar (demerara gives a more nuanced flavor, but if you're concerned about appearances, then white sugar gives you a clearer syrup)
4 cups or 1 part water

Heat the water and sugar in a small pot over medium heat. Stir until the sugar is completely dissolved and the liquid appears glassy. Let cool. The syrup will usually keep for about a week. If you add 1 tbsp of vodka, then it will last an entire month.

ritz cocktail

Flaming the garnish makes this a much more impressive drink. To flame the peel, cut a disc of peel off a room-temperature orange with a paring knife, taking as little white pith with it as possible. Hold the peel between the thumb and fingers of one hand, and light a match with the other. Warm the peel to draw out its oils, then place the match between the peel and the top of the drink and quickly squeeze the peel. The oils should flame across the drink and add their flavors to it. Practice this technique before attempting to show it off.

1 oz cognac
½ oz Cointreau
¼ oz maraschino liqueur
¼ oz lemon juice
champagne
flamed orange peel for garnish

Combine the first four ingredients in a mixing glass and stir with ice. Strain into a martini glass and fill with champagne. Garnish with the peel.

salty dog

makes 1 drink

As Kingsley Amis puts it, "You either like it or not." Try it with vodka if you're on the fence, but the gin, grapefruit, and salt make for a surprisingly appetizing mix.

Balance the saltiness of the drink with a sweet dish such as Vanilla Bourbon French Toast (recipe on p. 95).

lemon or lime wedge
  for rimming
salt
1½ oz gin
3 oz fresh grapefruit juice

Moisten the rim of a rocks glass with the wedge and press the rim into a plate of salt. Add the gin, grapefruit juice, and ice, and then stir.

saratoga cocktail *makes 1 drink*

There is another cocktail also called the Saratoga, which includes whiskey, brandy, bitters, and vermouth but no fruit or champagne, which pre-dates this one by several long decades. That doesn't mean we must ignore this one; it just needs a new name. But you'll need to try it while you consider the question. It's only fair.

3–4 1-inch cubes of pineapple
2 strawberries, plus extra
    for garnish
¼ oz maraschino liqueur
3 dashes Angostura bitters
½ oz Simple Syrup
1½ oz cognac
champagne for floating
lemon peel for garnish

Muddle the fruit in a mixing glass with the liqueur, bitters, and syrup. Add the cognac and ice, and shake. Strain over fresh ice in a stem glass and top with champagne. Garnish with strawberries and lemon peel.

sea breeze

makes 1 drink

A child from the Cape Codder family.

Pair this tall drink with
Vanilla Bourbon French Toast.

1 ½ oz vodka
4 oz grapefruit juice
1 ½ oz cranberry juice
lime wedge for garnish

In a highball glass over ice, build the drink in the
order of the ingredients listed above.
Garnish with the lime.

vanilla bourbon french toast
serves 10–12

This recipe draws from French toast recipes in both Albert Schmid's *The Kentucky Bourbon Cookbook* and Marc Meyer and Peter Meehan's *Brunch*. The bourbon and vanilla combine to give this a headier flavor than your usual French toast.

2 cups whole milk
⅓ cup bourbon
5 eggs
½ cup sugar
2 tsp ground cinnamon
1 tsp vanilla extract
1 tbsp butter
12 slices challah bread

Mix the milk, bourbon, eggs, sugar, cinnamon, and vanilla in a bowl. In a hot skillet, melt a pat of butter. Dip the bread in the mix and cook in the skillet. Brown both sides. Serve with your choice of powdered sugar, maple syrup, or fruit.

tequila sunrise

The Biltmore Hotel in Phoenix, Arizona, is keen to remind us that its bartender invented the first Tequila Sunrise sometime in the 1930s or 1940s. However, that particular recipe—1¼ oz white tequila, ¾ oz crème de cassis, lime juice, and club soda, all in a highball glass with ice—shares only a general outline with the recipe most of us know. The OJ, grenadine, and tequila standard has a later-origin story, and on its side sit the Rolling Stones. Bobby Lazoff claims to have invented the current version in the early 1970s, while he was working the bar at Sausalito's Trident, a hip club owned by the Kingston Trio (bet you weren't expecting that, were you?). During a launch party for the Stones's 1972 tour, Lazoff served his specialty tequila drink to Mick Jagger, who then spread the recipe across the country.

1 ½ oz white tequila
4 or 5 oz orange juice
½ oz grenadine

In a highball glass filled with ice, add the tequila and then the orange juice, and float the grenadine on top of the drink.

valencia

makes 1 drink

Created by Frank Meier of the Ritz Bar, Paris.

½ oz apricot liqueur
1 oz orange juice
5–6 oz champagne
orange twist for garnish

Pour the liqueur and the juice in a champagne
flute, and top with champagne. Garnish with
the twist.

In victory
we deserve it,
in defeat
we need it.

—Winston Churchill,
on champagne

white sangria

makes 8 drinks

This recipe for a sweet, sparkling sangria comes from the *New York Times* and seems like the perfect accompaniment to a lazy morning spent reading the Sunday paper, though it may not improve your crossword performance.

Serve with a strata, quiche, or other easy-to-serve egg dish.

1 small pear or green apple, chopped
1 small navel orange, peeled and chopped
1 bottle sparkling wine
1¾ cups apple juice
1⅓ cups Cointreau
1 cup club soda

Place the fruit in a pitcher. Follow with your wine, juice, and Cointreau.
Let sit for an hour or so in your refrigerator, and when you're ready to serve,
add the club soda and stir. Serve in glasses with ice and include a few
pieces of the fruit with each serving.

the
bloody
mary
and beyond

You can mix it so it will taste as though it had absolutely no alcohol of any kind in it and a glass of it will still have as much kick as a really good big martini.

—Ernest Hemingway,
on the Bloody Mary

Bloody Marys dominate the brunch cocktail roster and rarely appear on a menu after five o'clock.

While you might order an Irish Coffee after a long dinner or mix a Mimosa at any hour, the Bloody Mary really only fits in next to a plate of Eggs Benedict (recipe on p. 151), huevos rancheros, or a Greek omelet. The spices, the tomato juice, the lemon juice, the liquor, and even the usual celery stick all combine into something that seems like a breakfast in itself. And since you get 100 percent of your recommended daily allowance of vitamin A and 25 percent of your vitamin C in just 6 ounces of tomato juice, a Bloody Mary is the rare drink that's actually (somewhat) healthy. Of course, its health benefits have always been secondary to more licentious concerns.

The Bloody Mary was invented in 1925 by Fernand "Pete" Petiot, the bartender at Harry's New York Bar. If you're wondering how a drink was invented during Prohibition, the answer lies in the fact that Harry's New York Bar was actually located in Paris, France, where it was founded by Harry McElhone. (And it's not in any way related to the Harry's Bar in Venice, where the Bellini first appeared.) Petiot wins out in the mixology race, thanks to his creation of not only the Bloody Mary but the French 75, the Side Car, and the unforgettably named Monkey Gland Cocktail.

Originally the drink included vodka, as you'd expect it today. When Petiot eventually moved to the United States to run an honest-to-god New York bar, in the St. Regis Hotel, he changed the spirit to gin due to a lack of vodka in the United States. At the insistence of the hotel's owners, the Astors, he also renamed it the Red Snapper. It wasn't until a successful campaign to introduce Smirnoff vodka to American drinkers in the 1960s that the original vodka version earned its place in the cocktail firmament. Just to confuse things, the comedian George Jessel, who was part of Smirnoff's campaign, appeared in an ad in which he facetiously claimed he was the drink's inventor in 1927, though he hedges it by saying, "If I wasn't the first ever, I was the happiest ever."

Petiot described his method of making the Bloody Mary as follows:

> I cover the bottom of the shaker with four large dashes of salt, two dashes of black pepper, two dashes of cayenne pepper, and a layer of Worcestershire sauce; I then add a dash of lemon juice and some cracked ice, put in two ounces of vodka and two ounces of thick tomato juice, shake, strain, and pour.

Not bad, but why stop there?

The **Bloody Mary** is a drink meant to be tinkered with, as it has been since it arrived in the States. I've included some classic variations as well as more modern approaches to this vegetable serving in a glass.

beer and
a smoke

makes 1 drink

This variation on a Michelada is from mixologist Jim Meehan of PDT.

Try it alongside huevos rancheros or a spicy omelet.

1 oz Sombra mezcal

¾ oz lime juice, freshly squeezed

dash Bitter Truth celery bitters

4 dashes Cholula hot sauce

kosher salt, celery salt, and black pepper for the rim

6 oz Victory pilsner

orange and lime zest for garnish

Combine the first four ingredients and stir with ice in a cocktail shaker. Rim a chilled collins glass with kosher salt, celery salt, and freshly ground black pepper. Strain the liquid into the glass, top with pilsner, and garnish with grated orange and lime zest.

the bloody bull

makes 1 drink

A classic brunch drink, this version of the recipe comes from Chris Hannah of French 75.

Pair this with bacon, fried eggs, and toast.

1½ oz vodka
4 oz Bloody Mary mix (see p. 113)
1 oz beef broth
2 olives
1 lemon wedge
2 pickled beans

Roll first three ingredients from mixing glass to highball glass,
finishing with the liquid in the highball glass. Add ice
and garnish with the remaining ingredients.

bloody butrum

makes 1 drink

While its history is unclear, I'd like to think this drink bears some relation to Hillous Butrum, a member of Hank Williams's band.

2 oz vodka
2 dashes celery salt
pinch of dill (dried)
2 dashes ground pepper
2 dashes Tabasco sauce
3 dashes Worcestershire sauce
4 oz Clamato Juice
2 lime wedges

In a mixing glass, combine the ingredients over ice and roll. Strain into a goblet or pint glass over ice.

homemade clamato-style juice

makes 1 pitcher

25 oz clam juice
46 oz tomato juice
salt and pepper to taste

Combine ingredients in a pitcher, mix, and chill.

bloody caesar

makes 1 drink

You might not guess it from the name, but this cocktail comes from Canada, where it was created in 1969 by Walter Chell.

2 oz vodka
3 oz Clamato Juice
¼ tsp horseradish
3 dashes hot sauce
3 dashes Worcestershire sauce
lemon wedge for garnish

Combine ingredients in a shaker with crushed ice. Shake and strain into a highball glass half-filled with fresh crushed ice. Garnish with a lemon wedge.

bloody maria

makes 1 drink

The tequila-based variation of the classic.

Try with a plate of Roast Beef Hash (recipe on p. 108).

2 oz silver tequila
4 oz tomato juice
½ tsp Worcestershire sauce
2 dashes Tabasco sauce
juice of ¼ lemon,
  freshly squeezed
pinch of celery salt
salt and black pepper to taste
celery stalk for garnish

Combine ingredients in a shaker with crushed ice, and stir well. Strain into a highball glass half-filled with ice cubes. Add garnish.

roast beef hash

serves 4

Most hash recipes opt for corned beef and white potatoes. This recipe, based on one by Heather Arndt Anderson, offers more interesting flavors thanks to the use of sweet potatoes and roast beef. You can buy the meat specifically for the hash—it's worth it—but making hash also offers a chance to use leftover roast. The paprika adds a spice to the potatoes' sweetness.

2 tbsp olive oil
1 zucchini, chopped
½ red onion, sliced
2 sweet potatoes, boiled and chopped
½ lb roast beef, chopped
½ tsp paprika
1 tsp thyme
salt and pepper to taste
4 eggs (1 per person)

In a large pan, heat the olive oil. Add the zucchini, onion, potatoes, beef, and paprika. Cook until browned and crispy at the edges. In a separate pan, fry an egg over easy. Serve the hash with the egg laid on top.

bloody marie

makes 1 drink

With the recent legalization of absinthe in the United States, you might consider using another brand of absinthe in place of the Pernod.

1 ½ oz vodka

3 oz tomato juice

1 tsp lemon juice, freshly squeezed

dash Worcestershire sauce

dash Tabasco sauce

dash Pernod absinthe

salt and freshly ground black pepper
  to taste

Combine all ingredients in a shaker with ice cubes. Shake well and strain into a rocks glass or tumbler with a cube of ice.

rolled, not shaken

Drinks that call for tomato juice should be "rolled" between the two sides of a Boston shaker or, failing that, any two large glasses. This method prevents the foaming that can be caused by shaking the mixture. (Drinks with beef broth, such as the Bloody Bull, are the exception. The broth thickens the tomato juice enough to prevent froth.) However, many of the original sources for the recipes in this chapter recommend shaking or stirring. I've followed the method called for by their creators, but if your drinks are turning up bubbly, then you might want to switch your mixing style.

bloody mary
(the standard)

makes 1 drink

There are many slight twists or variations on the recipe, but if you set a glass of the following before any drinker, he or she would recognize it as your classic Bloody Mary.

2 oz vodka

3 oz tomato juice or V8 juice

juice of half a lemon, freshly squeezed

6 dashes Worcestershire sauce

5 dashes Tabasco sauce

salt, pepper, and horseradish to taste

celery stalk and lemon wedge for garnish

This concoction can be shaken, rolled, or stirred, depending on your inclination, and then poured in a tall glass over ice cubes. Garnish it with the celery stalk and lemon wedge.

how to make
your own mixes

You can find premade mixes in most supermarkets,
but a homemade mix shares the same benefits
as freshly squeezed orange juice or homemade sour mix:
fewer sugars and preservatives. Always expect your guests
to experiment with their own flavors, but starting off
with a flavored mix like one of these will prime the pump.

bloody mary mix
makes 1 quart

1 quart store-bought or homemade
tomato juice (recipe on p. 114)
or vegetable juice
2 tbsp Worcestershire sauce
1 tbsp lime or lemon juice,
freshly squeezed
¼ tsp bar sugar
¼ tsp black pepper
¼ tsp hot sauce
⅛ tsp garlic powder
celery sticks or lime wheels
for garnish

Mix the ingredients in a pitcher and keep
chilled. For a simple **Bloody Mary**, combine 3
or 4 parts of this mix with 1 part vodka in a tall
glass of ice cubes. Stir and add garnish.

homemade V8-style juice
(via dale degroff)
makes 1 pitcher

46 oz tomato juice
4 oz celery juice
4 oz carrot juice
4 oz green pepper juice
4 oz red pepper juice
2 oz onion juice
2 oz fennel juice
salt and pepper to taste

In a pitcher, combine the ingredients,
mix, and chill.

spicy tomato juice

makes 1 pitcher

2½ oz lemon juice

2 tsp Tabasco sauce

1 tsp Worcestershire sauce

46 oz tomato juice

salt and pepper to taste

Combine the ingredients in a pitcher and mix well before chilling in the refrigerator.

tomato juice

makes 1 quart

16 medium tomatoes, cored
    and quartered, or 2 28-oz cans
    of tomatoes

1 cup water

½ medium onion, chopped

2 ribs of celery, chopped

6 sprigs of parsley, minced

½ tsp paprika

1 tsp sugar

2 tsp salt

freshly ground black pepper to taste

Combine your tomatoes, water, onion, celery, and parsley together in a large saucepan. Once you've brought it to a boil, reduce the heat and let it simmer for a ½ hour. Put the resulting mixture through a food mill or, if you don't have a food mill, separate the liquid from the solids with a strainer. Once you have your juice, mix in the paprika, sugar, and salt. Add pepper to taste. Chill until breakfast is ready.

tomato puree

makes 1 gallon

6 lbs tomatoes, cored and quartered

In a large pot filled with enough water to cover them, cook the tomatoes over medium heat for 15 minutes or until soft. Take the pot off the heat, and pour the tomatoes into a strainer over a large bowl and let cool (you may have to work in batches). Refrigerate the juice that collects in the bowl, then run the tomatoes through a food mill or fine strainer to remove the skins and seeds. Combine refrigerated juice and tomatoes.

bloody mary
(dickson's version)
makes 1 drink

While it's unclear who Dickson was, we do know one thing about him: he liked his Bloody Marys spicy.

 Match it with a frittata.

2 oz chili-infused vodka
1 oz fino sherry
7 oz tomato juice
1 oz lemon juice, freshly squeezed
2–3 dashes Tabasco sauce
½ oz Worcestershire sauce
½ tsp horseradish
1 tsp celery salt
salt and pepper to taste
celery stalk, stuffed green olives,
    and cherry tomato for garnish

Add vodka, sherry, and tomato juice to a shaker of cracked ice. Stir well. Add lemon juice, Tabasco sauce, Worcestershire sauce, and horseradish, and stir again. Add celery salt, salt, and pepper, and stir until the drink is chilled. Strain into a highball glass half-filled with ice cubes. Add garnish.

how to make
chili-infused vodka

makes 2 cups

This infused vodka is perfectly suited for a spicy Bloody Mary. The choice of pepper, jalapeño or otherwise, depends on the level of spiciness you're aiming for. While store-bought versions such as Absolut Peppar are perfectly acceptable, making your own infusion offers a chance to tailor the flavor to personal taste.

6 ripe chili peppers

2 cups vodka

Combine 5 of the whole chilies and the vodka in a sealable jar or bottle. Cut the 6th chili in half lengthwise and add both halves to the vodka as well. Seal and leave for at least 8 hours. Strain out the chilies when it's hot enough for your taste.

bloody mary
(the Employees Only version)

This variation comes from *Speakeasy*, the excellent book by the owners of Manhattan bar Employees Only. It uses horseradish as well as hot sauce for the drink's bite.

Try it with a Full English Breakfast Quiche (recipe on pp. 120–121).

for the mix

makes 1 quart

3 cups tomato juice
½ tbsp capers, crushed
3 oz Worcestershire sauce
2 oz lemon juice, freshly squeezed
1 oz olive brine
½ tsp celery salt
1 tsp black pepper, freshly ground
1 tsp Tabasco sauce
4 tbsp horseradish, freshly grated

Combine all ingredients and stir well. Refrigerate overnight, and stir again before using.

for the drink

makes 1 drink

5 oz mix
2 oz Russian Standard vodka
½ oz lemon juice
celery stalk, lemon wedge, skewered
  grape tomato, pickled onion,
  and olive for garnish

Roll the mix and vodka with ice, and then pour into a large glass over fresh ice. Add lemon juice and garnish.

the full english breakfast quiche

makes one 10-inch quiche

The "full English" is an unstoppable hangover cure. Fried eggs, sausage, bacon, mushrooms, and tomatoes, and often whatever else you decide to toss into your skillet. As author W. Somerset Maugham said, "To eat well in England you should have breakfast three times a day." This quiche delivers the best of British cuisine all in one delicious slice.

This recipe was adapted from British website AllAboutYou.com and uses a tweaked version of Mark Bittman's tart crust in *How to Cook Everything*. Feel free to substitute your own crust recipe (or go with store-bought if you're having a rough morning), but try to use a butter-based one. It is, after all, the stand-in for the toast.

for the crust

1¼ cup plain flour
½ tsp salt
1 tsp English mustard powder, such as Colman's
10 tbsp butter, chilled and cubed
1 egg yolk
3 tbsp ice water, or more if needed

for the filling

4 pork sausages
½ lb cherry tomatoes, halved
½ lb bacon lardons
½ lb button mushrooms, halved
1 tbsp olive oil
½ pt crème fraîche
3 eggs, beaten
1 tsp English mustard powder

Preheat the oven to 370°F. In a food processor, pulse the flour, salt, and mustard powder a couple times before adding the butter. Process until mixed (about 10 seconds). Add the yolk and process a few seconds longer, then transfer to a bowl and add the water. Use your hands to mix in the water, and then shape into a ball. Put it in the freezer for 10 minutes.

Using plenty of flour, sprinkle the countertop, the roller, and then the dough. Roll out the dough to ⅛-inch thick. Line a 10-inch fluted, removable-bottom tart pan with the dough, allowing some to hang over the edges, and press the dough into the edges of the pan. Refrigerate for about 1 hour.

Put the sausages in a roasting pan and place in the oven for 10 minutes. Then remove the pan from the oven and add the tomatoes, bacon, and mushrooms, all topped with the olive oil. Put the pan back into the oven for 15–20 minutes.

Remove the dough from the fridge and prick with the tines of a fork, cover with parchment paper, and then place pie weights on top. Bake for 8 minutes. Remove from oven and take off the weights and paper. Turn down the oven to 300°F and put the pan back in the oven for 2–3 minutes to dry out.

Remove the pan from the oven. Slice the sausages and combine the pieces with the bacon, mushrooms, and tomatoes. Scatter these ingredients in the pan. Mix the crème fraîche, eggs, and mustard powder, and pour over your other ingredients in the pan. Bake 30–35 minutes, until the mixture is set, and then turn off the oven, open its door, and allow the quiche to cool in the oven 15 more minutes. Serve hot or cold.

the bullshot

makes 1 drink

Don't be put off by the name. This is a vegetarian-unfriendly twist on a Bloody Mary that skips the tomato juice in favor of a meatier choice.

○
○ Switch the vodka for rum for the **Creole variation**.

2 oz vodka

4 oz cold beef consommé or stock

½ oz lemon juice, freshly squeezed

¼ oz Worcestershire sauce

2 dashes Tabasco sauce

pinch of celery salt

pinch of cayenne pepper

Stir all ingredients with ice in a shaker, and then strain into a highball glass half-filled with ice.

eggs
and bacon

makes 1 drink

Created by cocktail consultant Charlotte Voisey for the Santa Monica, California, restaurant FIG, this cocktail doesn't so much accompany your brunch as become your brunch.

3 oz Bacon-Infused Gin (recipe on p. 139)
2 oz egg whites
1 oz lemon juice, freshly squeezed
1 oz orange-blossom honey
crispy piece of applewood-smoked bacon
for garnish

Combine ingredients in a shaker with crushed ice and shake well. Strain over ice into a double rocks glass and lay the crispy strip of bacon across the top of the glass.

geisha whirl

makes 1 drink

The soy sauce and wasabi variation offers a change from the standard Worcestershire sauce and horseradish.

1½ oz vodka
3 oz tomato juice
1 tsp lemon juice, freshly squeezed
dash salt
dash soy sauce
dash Tabasco sauce
½ tsp wasabi, or to taste

Combine ingredients in a shaker with crushed ice. Roll and strain into a tumbler or rocks glass half-filled with ice cubes.

the green mary

makes 1 drink

This recipe, from New York City restaurant Cafeteria, switches the shade of the traditional drink.

Try this dense, sharply flavored cocktail with a light Watermelon, Feta, and Red Onion Salad (recipe on p. 128).

for the green mix

1 cup yellow tomatoes, chopped
1 cup tomatillos, husks removed
1 cup cucumber, peeled and chopped
1 cup green apple, peeled and chopped

Combine ingredients in equal parts in a blender and puree until smooth.

for the drink

6 oz green mix
1½ oz vodka
½ oz lime juice, freshly squeezed
3–4 dashes green jalapeño Tabasco sauce
½ tsp horseradish
¼ tsp celery seed
1 splash olive juice
celery heart, cucumber slices, lime, green olives, and salt and pepper for garnish

Combine the green mix with the rest of the ingredients in a shaker with ice. Roll and strain into a 12-oz glass. Garnish with celery heart, cucumber slices, lime, green olives, and a sprinkling of salt and pepper.

watermelon, feta, and red onion salad

serves 4

One of the risks with bloodys as a category of cocktail is that, with all that thick juice, you end up not quite hungry enough to really eat anything. Down that path lies danger, and maybe a second hangover. While this recipe's origins aren't impressive—the creator seems to be one "ElaineHN" online—this is an ideal recipe to pair with a heavier, spicy drink.

½ red onion, chopped
juice of ½ lime
1 tbsp balsamic vinegar
¼ watermelon, cubed
2 oz feta cheese, cubed
1½ tbsp basil, chopped

In a small bowl, combine the onion, lime juice, and vinegar to create your dressing. In a large salad bowl, toss the watermelon, feta, and dressing, then top with the chopped basil.

krauter

makes 1 drink

For the many drinkers looking for the taste of sauerkraut in their cocktail.

1½ oz vodka
1½ oz tomato juice
1½ oz sauerkraut juice
1 tsp lemon juice, freshly squeezed
dash salt
dash Worcestershire sauce
dash Tabasco sauce

Combine ingredients in a shaker with crushed ice. Shake well and strain into a tumbler or rocks glass half-filled with ice cubes.

the mad bull

makes 1 drink

The aquavit, a Scandinavian spirit, makes all the difference in this drink.

1½ oz aquavit
¾ oz lime juice, freshly squeezed
2 oz tomato juice
1 oz beef consommé or stock
celery salt for garnish

Combine ingredients in a shaker with ice and shake well. Strain into a highball glass and garnish with celery salt.

maple bacon bloody mary

makes 1 drink

This combination of brunch flavors was created by Marcia Simmons of DrinkoftheWeek.com. She recommends using freshly made tomato juice.

To add to the bacon flavor, consider a Bacon-Infused Vodka (recipe on p. 139).

1½ oz vodka
4 oz tomato juice
3 dashes Worcestershire sauce
¼ oz lemon juice
¼ tsp horseradish
1 tsp maple syrup
salt and pepper to taste
1 cooked bacon strip for garnish

In a double rocks glass partly filled with ice cubes, add the ingredients and stir. Garnish with the bacon.

michelada

makes 1 drink

Not as alcoholic as the Bloody Mary, the Michelada is a useful way to spruce up a light beer such as Corona, Negra Modelo, or Tecate. Without the tomato juice, this is called a **Chelada**.

○ ○ Pair with Scrambled Egg Enchiladas with Black Bean Sauce (recipe on p. 132).

1 oz lime juice, freshly squeezed
salt for rim of glass
1 12-oz bottle of beer
2 dashes Maggi Seasoning (if you can't find this Mexican product,
opt for Worcestershire or soy sauce)
2 dashes Cholula or Tapatío hot sauce
1–3 oz tomato juice
lime wedge for garnish

Moisten the rim of a chilled beer glass with a lime, then salt the rim.
Combine the ingredients in the glass. Garnish with a lime wedge.

scrambled egg enchiladas with black bean sauce

serves 6

If you aren't a devotee of chipotle chilies in adobo sauce, you're about to become one. The smoky, slow burn pairs perfectly with the creaminess of the eggs and cheese in this breakfast version of a Mexican favorite. This recipe was created by Rick Bayless and appeared, amazingly, in *Men's Health*.

2 tbsp vegetable oil
½ small onion, cut into ¼-inch slices
2 cloves garlic, chopped
1 can (15 oz) black beans in liquid
1 cup water
1 can chopped chipotle chili peppers
  in adobo sauce
1½ tsp salt
6 corn tortillas
4 scallions, thinly sliced
7 eggs
3 oz reduced-fat cream cheese, cubed
⅔ cup shredded Chihuahua or cheddar cheese
2 tbsp cilantro, chopped

Preheat the oven to 400°F. In a large skillet, heat 1 tablespoon of the oil. Add the onion slices and cook until golden, about 7 minutes. Add the garlic and cook for another minute. Put the onion and garlic in a blender, leaving the oil in the pan but taking the pan off the stove. In the blender, add the beans, water, peppers, and ¾ teaspoon of the salt, then puree the sauce.

On a baking sheet, lay out the tortillas and coat them with oil on both sides, and then stack them in pairs. Bake for about 3 minutes, then stack them all together and keep warm.

Return the pan to medium heat and add another tablespoon of oil as well as the sliced scallions. Cook for 2–3 minutes, until soft. In a bowl, whisk the eggs and ¾ teaspoon salt. Add to the pan, stirring consistently until the eggs are only just set. Remove the pan from the heat and stir in the cream cheese.

Pour ½ cup of the sauce into a 9-inch-by-9-inch baking dish. Fill each tortilla with the egg and cream cheese mixture and roll them up individually, then arrange them side by side in the baking dish. Cover with the remaining sauce. Top with the shredded cheese. Bake for 10–12 minutes. Sprinkle with the chopped cilantro before serving.

the bloody mary buffet

Nearly everyone who drinks Bloody Marys believes that only they can get the recipe right. And so why not let them try? Dale DeGroff suggests in *The Craft of the Cocktail* that you offer a make-your-own Bloody Mary spread rather than a single, uniform drink. Some will make theirs extra spicy, some will want extra olives, and some will just stick to juice.

Set out multiple juices, a bowl of ice, and bottles of vodka, tequila, gin, and aquavit. Besides these, you can include any number of garnishes, such as:

carrot sticks
celery
cocktail onions
cucumber spears
elephant caper berries
fennel (baby or dried)

herbs (such as dill, basil, and oregano)
horseradish, fresh, skinned, and cut for grating
hot sauces (such as Tabasco and Cholula)
lemon wedges
lime wedges
Old Bay Seasoning
olives
pepper (black and cayenne)
peppers
radishes
salt (kosher and celery)
scallions
shellfish (such as clams, oysters, and shrimp)
Tomolives
Worcestershire sauce

And anything else you think your guests will like. You want Slim Jims in your drink? Go for it. Pickled beets? I can't stop you. Creamed pickled herring? You want people to enjoy this party, don't you?

red snapper

makes 1 drink

The gin-based variation on the Bloody Mary that introduced Americans to the drink.

3 oz gin

4 dashes Worcestershire sauce

8 dashes Tabasco sauce

2 pinches of salt and pepper

½ oz lemon juice

8 oz tomato juice

lemon wedge for garnish

Roll the ingredients in a mixing glass, and strain into a pint glass
filled three quarters of the way with ice. Add garnish.

sangrita

makes 8 glasses

This is what happens when the tequila and the tomato juice in a Bloody Maria split up.

1 lb ripe tomatoes or 1 14-oz can chopped tomatoes
1 small onion, finely chopped
2 small green chilies, seeded and chopped
4 oz orange juice, freshly squeezed
juice of 3 limes, freshly squeezed
½ tsp bar sugar
pinch of salt
1 shot gold tequila

If using fresh tomatoes, cut a cross at the base of each tomato. Place them in a heatproof bowl and cover in boiling water. Let sit for 3 minutes. Remove tomatoes with a slotted spoon and place in a bowl of cold water. Remove the skins, then cut in halves and remove seeds. Chop tomatoes and put them in a food processor.

If using either canned or fresh tomatoes, combine chopped tomatoes, onion, chilies, orange juice, lime juice, sugar, and salt in food processor. Process until smooth, then transfer to a pitcher and chill for at least an hour.

Serve in a glass over ice with a shot glass of gold tequila on the side.

the beer back

My first introduction to the beer back was beside a spicy Bloody Mary from Park Slope's Applewood restaurant. The bartender had supplied a short glass of Kelso to offset the primary drink's spiciness. Applewood isn't the only place where you can find this innovation. *Food Republic* reports that Chicago's Dunlays on Clark backs up its bloodys with shorts of Guinness. It's a smart way to prevent you from gulping down the Bloody Mary, hoping to cool off your tongue but only making it hotter. And if your preferred brunch place doesn't do it automatically, it's an easy addition to your order.

Midmorning was the first well-established masculine cocktail hour.

—Lucius Beebe,
The Stork Club Bar Book

137

smoked martinez

makes 1 drink

An original recipe that shakes up the classic Martinez with the addition of bacon and maple syrup.

1 tsp maple syrup
1 oz Bacon-Infused Gin
2 oz sweet vermouth
dash orange bitters

Combine the ingredients in a cocktail shaker with ice. Shake and strain into a chilled cocktail glass.

how to make bacon-infused spirits

makes 1 pint

Nothing says breakfast drinking like bacon-infused booze. While the Eggs and Bacon and the Smoked Martinez in this book both choose gin as the base spirit, you could easily use these instructions with any liquor. Also, the ratio of bacon-to-alcohol can be entirely up to you. But pay close attention to the instructions for filtering; otherwise you'll end up with too much fat in your drink.

½ tbsp butter
3 strips bacon
1 pint gin or other liquor

Cook the bacon in a pan with butter, then pour the entire contents of the pan into a jar filled with your liquor. Seal the jar, and leave it for 6 hours. Then remove the strips of bacon, reseal the jar, and place it in the freezer overnight. The fat will freeze but the spirit will not. Remove the "fat cap" and then strain through cheesecloth into another jar. (You may want to repeat the freezing process more than once.)

tomato juice cocktail

makes 1 drink

Before you go to too much trouble, this a soft drink. But if it weren't for Frank Meier at the Ritz Bar, who was known for these cocktails in Paris after World War I, Petiot may never have had the inspiration to spike tomato juice with vodka.

1 large ripe tomato
celery salt to taste
½ tsp Worcestershire sauce

Crush the tomato in a shaker, then add the salt and sauce. Shake well and strain into a double cocktail glass.

tomato martini

makes 1 drink

As if you asked for your Bloody Mary with "no pulp."

3 oz Tomato-Infused Gin
1½ oz dry vermouth
2 dashes Lillet Blanc
cherry tomato for garnish

Stir the ingredients with ice and strain into a chilled cocktail glass. Garnish with a cherry tomato.

tomato-infused gin

16 oz London dry gin
1 lb ripe tomatoes or cherry tomatoes

Chop the tomato and put in a glass jar, and then add the gin.
Allow one or two days for it to steep, tasting occasionally.
Once it's achieved the desired strength, strain while
pressing gently to release the liquid.

the science of the bloody mary

In 2011, Neil C. Da Costa, PhD, a flavor analytical chemist, presented to the American Chemical Society an analysis of the chemical reactions that take place after a Bloody Mary's preparation. Though the ACS did not mention at what time of day this meeting took place—I hope around noon—Da Costa did propose some of these basic rules for a good Bloody Mary, as outlined in an official release by the American Chemical Society:

make it fresh. Chemically, the Bloody Mary is a "highly unstable" concoction and the quality tends to deteriorate quickly.

ice it up. Serving Bloody Marys on ice helps to slow down the chemical reactions involving acids in tomato juice and other ingredients that degrade the taste.

mind your mixes. If you use a cocktail mix, add some fresh ingredients to enhance the flavor and aroma.

splurge on the juice. Tomato juice makes up most of the Bloody Mary's volume, so use high-quality juice that has a deep, rich flavor.

economize on the vodka. The intense, spicy flavor of a Bloody Mary masks the vodka and using premium vodka makes little sense.

hangover
cures for the
morning after

Stay
drunk!

—Dean Martin,
on how to avoid
a hangover

A certain best-selling author I spoke with told me of a friend who was convinced **hangovers** are not caused by alcohol but by guilt.

He'd resolved never to feel guilty for getting drunk and had enjoyed a hangover-free life. Coming from a Catholic household, it's impossible for me to test his theory.

There have been dozens of articles investigating the medical and mythical cures for hangovers. These perhaps say more about the interests of journalists than they do about any great discoveries in the study of veisalgia (the technical term). Still, it seems as if people have searched fruitlessly for a foolproof hangover cure since the morning after alcohol was discovered. Ancient Assyrians ground swallows' beaks and drank them in myrrh, the Greeks whipped themselves until they bled out the alcohol, and the Romans opted for a fried canary.

We've found slightly more pleasant options since, I'm relieved to say. *Good* magazine suggests a quick, vigorous roll in the hay, provided your previous evening went well enough that you've awakened in the hay beside a willing partner. Since that option is unlikely to take place while *at* brunch, there are plenty of solutions to be found in a glass as well. Since 1546, the concept of "hair of the dog" has offered drinkers the preferred method of restoring their good spirits. Why fry up Tweety Bird when you can have a Corpse Reviver instead?

No matter how acute,
the pain of hangovers
can't rise above farce.

—Jim Harrison,
Off to the Side:
A Memoir

bartender's breakfast

makes 1 drink

Not just a hangover cure, but also the first meal of the day.

1 oz vodka
handful cherry tomatoes
1 leaf basil
pinch of ground coriander
pinch of celery salt
sprinkling of chopped chives
pinch of black pepper
cherry tomato and basil leaf
   for garnish

Add the ingredients to a blender without ice. Blend until smooth, then strain into a highball glass with ice. Garnish with a cherry tomato and basil leaf on a stick.

blood transfusion

A creation of bartender Salvatore Calabrese of London.

1 oz vodka

1 oz dry sherry

½ oz tomato juice

1 oz lime juice

pinch of celery salt

2 dashes Worcestershire sauce

1 oz Fernet Branca

In a highball glass with ice, pour first the vodka and sherry. Follow with the tomato and lime juices, then the celery salt and Worcestershire. Stir. Float the Fernet Branca on top.

The wrath of grapes.

—Jeffrey Bernard, journalist, on hangovers

the corpse reviver no. 1

makes 1 drink

This recipe comes from the classic *Savoy Cocktail Book.*

Consume along with a fortifying
plate of steak and eggs.

2 oz brandy

1 oz apple brandy or calvados

1 oz sweet vermouth

Combine ingredients in a shaker with ice.
Stir, strain, and serve in a chilled cocktail glass.

the corpse reviver no. 2

makes 1 drink

In case Number One didn't have the intended effect.

1 oz dry gin
1 oz Cointreau
1 oz Lillet Blanc
1 oz lemon juice
dash absinthe or Pernod
maraschino cherry for garnish

Combined all liquids with ice in a shaker. Once shaken, strain into a cocktail glass and garnish.

how to make jalapeño-infused agave nectar

makes 1 quart

3 medium-sized jalapeños, diced
20 oz agave nectar
10 oz water

Steep the jalapeños in 10 oz of simmering water for 5 minutes. Strain the jalapeños and add the remaining water to the agave nectar. Cool and refrigerate.

english heat

makes 1 drink

Created by New York–based bartender Leo Robitschek of NoMad NYC. Tuaca is a vanilla-and-citrus-flavored liqueur.

Pair with Eggs Benedict.

1½ oz London dry gin
¾ oz Dolin de Chambray
   dry vermouth
¾ oz Jalapeño-Infused Agave Nectar
1 oz lemon juice
¼ oz Tuaca

Combine all ingredients in a shaker, add ice, shake, and strain into a cocktail glass

eggs benedict

serves 4

This now-classic brunch meal was created by Lemuel Benedict and popularized at the Waldorf-Astoria Hotel, where he requested the combination as a cure for his pain. Below is an adaptation of *Saveur*'s take, based on the Waldorf-Astoria's recipe.

for the eggs

salt
2 tbsp white vinegar
2 tbsp butter
4 eggs
2 English muffins, split
4 slices Canadian bacon

for the hollandaise sauce

12 tbsp unsalted butter
3 egg yolks
2–3 tbsp lemon juice, freshly squeezed
salt and white pepper to taste

Bring a skillet of salted water to a simmer over medium heat, then add the vinegar. Crack each egg and keep in separate bowls. Add them to the water carefully so as not to break the yolk. Cover the skillet, and turn off the heat. Cook the eggs until the whites have firmed, or about 4 minutes. Remove them from the water and place them in a bowl of ice water.

Preheat the oven to 200°F—you'll be keeping things warm while you build the rest of the dish. First toast the muffins, then spread each with butter. Use the rest of the butter to fry the bacon in a pan until brown, or about 5 minutes, then place one slice on each muffin and return to the oven.

To make the hollandaise, start by melting butter in a separate pan over low heat. In a large saucepan, whisk together the eggs, lemon juice, 1 tbsp water, and salt and pepper until the mixture looks pale yellow in color before placing on a burner. Set the heat to medium-low, place the saucepan on the burner, and continue whisking until the whisk leaves trails in the eggs, or about 5 minutes. Remove the pan from the stove and begin whisking in the butter 1 tbsp at a time. Salt and pepper to taste.

Once the sauce is ready, reheat the eggs in a skillet of water for about a minute. Use a slotted spoon to place the eggs on towels to drain. Remove the muffins and bacon from the oven, and place an egg on top of each muffin. Once plated, spoon the sauce on top.

evelyn waugh's noonday reviver

makes 1 drink

"I cannot vouch for the authenticity of the attribution," writes Kingsley Amis. "But the mixture will certainly revive you, or something." No matter. Waugh had more than one hangover cure credited to him, likely because he found so many opportunities to test them out. Or something.

Amis recommends taking two of these at most, which for most of us should translate to one. For those who shrink at the sight of the gin bottle, substitute dark rum.

2 oz gin
½ pint Guinness
ginger beer

Put the gin and Guinness in a pint glass and fill to the top with ginger beer.

When I was younger, I made it a rule never to take strong drink before lunch. It is now my rule never to do so before breakfast.

—Winston Churchill

how to make orgeat syrup

makes about 1 cup

This almond-flavored syrup is a staple for tiki drinks such as the Mai Tai. It's becoming easier to find in many liquor stores and bars, but it can also easily be prepared and stored at home.

8 oz sliced almonds
1½ cups sugar
1 cup water
3 dashes orange-blossom water

Preheat your oven to 400°F. Toast the sliced almonds for 5 minutes, then allow them to cool before pulverizing in a blender or food processor. As you would with simple syrup, combine the sugar and water in a saucepan and bring to a boil. Add the almonds, simmer, and then remove from heat once the mixture reaches a boil again. Cover and let sit for at least 3 hours. Afterward, strain through cheesecloth into a bottle or jar. Add orange-blossom water and shake, and add 1 tbsp of vodka if you would like the syrup to last longer (and who wouldn't?). Otherwise, it will last for about a month.

fog-cutter

makes 1 drink

"The great utility of rum has given it the medical name of an antifogmatic," wrote an anonymous sage in *Massachusetts Spy* in 1789. "The quantity taken every morning is in exact proportion to the thickness of the fog." The drinks have gotten more interesting, but otherwise not much has changed since.

2 oz light rum
1 oz gin
1 oz brandy
1½ oz lemon juice
1 oz orange juice
½ tsp Orgeat Syrup
float of sweet sherry

In a shaker, combine all ingredients except sherry, shake with ice, and strain over fresh ice cubes in a highball glass. Add a float of sweet sherry on top.

london fog

makes 1 drink

Actor Burgess Meredith (you may know him as either the Penguin who fought Adam West's Batman, Rocky's trainer, or a member of Hollywood's blacklist) recommended this restorative. To "frappé" a drink means to serve the liquid over crushed or shaved ice.

1½ oz gin
¼ oz Pernod

Combine the gin and Pernod in a shaker, shake and frappé, and serve in a cocktail glass.

love in the ruins

makes 1 drink

This recipe comes from National Book Award–winning author Walker Percy's science-fiction novel *Love in the Ruins*, as prescribed by protagonist Dr. Tom More.

1 cup Tang, warm
2 duck eggs
2 oz vodka
1 dash Tabasco sauce

Combine all ingredients in a highball glass and consume while lying on the floor.

the parkeroo

The only real cure
for a hangover is death.

—Robert Benchley

"While painting a picket fence around my house,"
says actor Willard Parker, "I discovered that after two
Parkeroos I could remain stationary and let the fence
revolve around the brush. This will give you an idea!"

2 oz dry sherry
1 oz tequila
lemon twist for garnish

In a mixing glass, pour the liquid over ice. Chill
and then pour into a chilled champagne glass.
Add garnish.

I feel like a midget
with muddy feet
has been walking
over my tongue
all night.

—W. C. Fields,
on his hangover

pick-me-up

makes 1 drink

Recommended by actor Jean Hersholt—and he should
know. After all, he played a doctor on TV.

Try this dry drink
with a Swiss cheese omelet.

1½ oz dry vermouth
1½ oz cherry brandy
¾ oz dry gin

Combine ingredients and shake with ice
and strain into a chilled cocktail glass. This drink
is to be served as cold as possible and is to be
drunk as quickly as possible.

prairie oyster no. 1

makes 1 drink

Not to be confused with Rocky Mountain oysters, this longtime hangover cure seems to operate on the assumption that a raw egg might actually be *good* for a greenish stomach. The egg should be swallowed whole (as if you had even considered chewing it).

1 egg
1½ oz brandy
dash Worcestershire sauce
salt to taste

Crack the eggshell without breaking the yolk, and transfer the whole egg to a wineglass. Add the brandy, Worcestershire sauce, and salt to taste.

prairie oyster no. 4

makes 1 drink

For drinkers with a preference for a sweet and spicy approach, this variation opts for port and pepper. Again, the yolk should be swallowed whole. (I've skipped the unappetizing Prairie Oyster Nos. 2 and 3.)

1 egg yolk
2 or 3 grinds of black pepper
1 tbsp Worcestershire sauce
1½ oz port
celery salt to taste

Separate the unbroken egg yolk from the white, and put the yolk in a wineglass. Add pepper, Worcestershire, port, and celery salt.

the red devil

makes 1 drink

This drink comes from the old Le Perigord Restaurant at New York's Sherry-Netherland Hotel.

2¼ oz Irish whiskey
1¾ oz clam juice
1¾ oz tomato juice
2–3 dashes Worcestershire sauce
pinch of ground pepper
½ oz lime juice
lemon wedge for garnish

Combine ingredients. Shake and strain into a rocks glass. Add garnish.

the suffering bar steward

makes 1 drink

Also known as the original Suffering Bastard, this drink was created by bartender Joe Scialom of the Shepherd's Head Hotel in Cairo, Egypt. He supposedly first mixed it during World War II when supplies of other liquors and spirits were limited. The hangovers continued after the war ended, and by 1950 *Time* magazine was reporting that "Egypt's favorite drink is called a Suffering Bastard."

1 oz gin
2 oz brandy
½ oz Rose's Lime Cordial
2 dashes Angostura bitters
4 oz ginger beer
orange slice and mint sprig for garnish

Shake all but the ginger beer in a shaker with ice, then stir in the ginger beer. Strain into a double old-fashioned glass and add garnish.

I hadn't the heart
to touch my breakfast.
I told Jeeves to drink it himself.

—P. G. Wodehouse,
Leave It to Jeeves

suffering bastard

makes 1 drink

Despite the confusion over the Suffering Bar Steward's name, there's another worthy drink that claims the name Suffering Bastard all to itself. Essentially it's a Mai Tai that includes orange juice, popularized by Trader Vic's, though the recipes consistently vary. Rich simple syrup is twice as saturated as regular simple syrup. See p. 90 for the recipe.

2 oz dark rum

1 oz overproof rum

dash orange curaçao

dash Orgeat Syrup

dash Rich Simple Syrup

juice of 1 lime

lime slice and mint sprig for garnish

Combine all the ingredients in a shaker with ice. Shake and strain into a double old-fashioned or Mai Tai glass filled with fresh ice. Add garnish.

acknowledgments

Thanks to

. . . editor Flannery Scott, publisher Rick Rinehart, publicity director Kalen Landow, production editor Janice Braunstein, designer Maria Kauffman, and everyone else at Taylor Trade for making this book happen.

. . . photographer Salma Khalil, who not only took the photos in this book but also saved me from the misguided plan to shoot the pictures myself.

. . . bartenders Derek Brown, St. John Frizell, Chris Hannah, Leo Robitschek, and Philip Ward for providing their own original recipes for this book.

. . . friends and often more-than-willing recipe testers Pepe Abola, Bobby Bannister, Natalie Be'er, Michael Camarra, Dave Clifford, Willie Davis, Shannon Derby, Brittany Flynn, Mandy Gabriel, Katie Gilligan, Alex and Andrea Hatziyannis, Seth Hersey, Philip Kiracofe, Andy Kokoszka, Kevin Lawler, David Maddy, J. Ross Marshall, Chris Miles, John Parsley, Andy Phillips, Nicole Raymond, David Ring, Cathy Snow, Leah Taylor, Alexandra Templer, Lukas Volger, Ashley Voroba, Brittany Woodell, and Nancy Wong.

. . . my parents, Andy, Carla, and Enzo.

And most of all, thanks to Katy Hershberger, for helping me make this happen, from the first idea to the final glass.

bibliography

Amis, Kingsley. *Everyday Drinking: The Distilled Kingsley Amis*. New York: Bloomsbury, 2008.

Anderson, Heather Arndt. "Roast Beef Hash." *Voodoo and Sauce*. Accessed November 7, 2011. http://voodooandsauce.com/?p=3423.

Bayless, Rick. "Scrambled Egg Enchiladas with Black Bean Sauce." *Men's Health*. Accessed November 5, 2011. http://recipes.menshealth.com /Recipe/scrambled-egg-enchiladas-with-black-bean-sauce.aspx.

Beebe, Lucius. *The Stork Club Bar Book*. New York: Rinehart & Company, 1946.

"Bellini." *CocktailDB*. Accessed August 13, 2011. http://www.cocktaildb.com /recipe_detail?id=4742.

Beringer, Guy. "Brunch: A Plea." *Hunter's Weekly*, 1895.

"The Biltmore Original Tequila Sunrise/Absolut-ly Wright Martini." The Wright Bar at the Arizona Biltmore. Accessed August 15, 2011. http://www.cocktailatlas.com/L2Signature/Arizona_Biltmore /Wright_Bar.htm.

Bissell, Tom. "The Last Lion." *Outside Magazine*. Accessed November 1, 2011. http://www.outsideonline.com/outdoor-adventure /celebrities/The-Last-Lion.html?page=3.

Bittman, Mark. *How to Cook Everything: 2,000 Simple Recipes for Great Food*. Hoboken, NJ: John Wiley & Sons, 2008.

"Bloody Mary Cocktail Timelines." *Twoop*. Accessed August 12, 2011. http://www.twoop.com/food/bloody-mary-cocktail.html.

"Bourbon French Toast Recipe." *Imbibe Magazine*. Accessed November 5, 2011. http://www.imbibemagazine.com/Bourbon-French-Toast-Recipe.

Buchanan, Rachel. "Shake, Shake." *The Age*. November 25, 1997. Accessed May 22, 2011. http://www.ladieshats.com.au/ladies-hats -articles/1997/11/25/shake-shake.

Burkhart, Jeff. "Barfly: When It's Not Just Another Tequila Sunrise." *San Jose Mercury News*. Accessed August 15, 2011. http://www.mercurynews.com/ci_18305167.

"Cafe Brulot Recipe." *Saveur*. Accessed May 22, 2011. http://www.saveur.com /article/Wine-and-Drink/Cafe-Brulot.

Calabrese, Salvatore. "Cocktail Recipes by Salvatore Calabrese Cocktail Bartender at Bar Fifty." Accessed August 14, 2011. http://www.salvatore-calabrese.co.uk/salvatore-calabrese -cocktail-recipes.html.

————. "Hangover Cures Recipes by Salvatore Calabrese Cocktail Maestro at Bar Fifty." Accessed August 14, 2011. http://www.salvatore -calabrese.co.uk/salvatore-calabrese-hangover-cures.html.

"Camel Juice." *CocktailDB*. Accessed September 15, 2011. http://cocktaildb.com/recipe_detail?id=407.

Castillo, Jenny. "Green Bloody Mary Recipe." *Food Republic*. Accessed June 18, 2011. http://www.foodrepublic.com/2011/04/21 /green-bloody-mary-recipe.

Chopra, Sanjiv, and Alan Lotvin with David Fisher. *Doctor Chopra Says: Medical Facts and Myths Everyone Should Know*. New York: St. Martin's Press, 2010.

Cole, Adam. "Cocktail Chemistry: Parsing the Bloody Mary." *NPR*. Accessed June 18, 2011. http://www.npr.org/blogs /health/2011/03/29/134931452/cocktail-chemistry-parsing -the-bloody-mary.

Collin, Rima, and Richard Collin. *The New Orleans Cookbook*. New York: Random House, 1987.

"The Corpse Reviver Family of Cocktails" *Oh Gosh*. Accessed September 13, 2011. http://ohgo.sh/archive/corpse-revivers.

Cram, Mildred. *Old Seaport Towns of the South*. New York: Dodd, Mead, 1917.

"Creating the Perfect Bloody Mary: Good Chemistry of Fresh Ingredients." American Chemical Society. Accessed November 3, 2011. http://portal.acs.org/portal/acs/corg/content?_nfpb=true&_pageLabel=PP_ARTICLEMAIN&node_id=222&content_id=CNBP_026943&use_sec=true&sec_url_var=region1&__uuid=04b35201-4465-46ab-b21c-7d712f578527.

Crumpacker, Bunny. *How to Slice an Onion: Cooking Basics and Beyond*. New York: Thomas Dunne/St. Martin's Press, 2009.

DeGroff, Dale. *The Craft of the Cocktail*. New York: Clarkson Potter, 2002.

Doesser, Linda. *Vodka: Invigorating Vodka Cocktails*. Bath: Parragon, 2009.

"Drink Recipes: Buck's Fizz." *Helium*. Accessed September 22, 2011. http://www.helium.com/items/848653-drink-recipes-bucks-fizz/print.

Dyer, Geoff. *Jeff in Venice, Death in Varanasi*. New York: Pantheon, 2009.

"Eggs Benedict Recipe." *Saveur*. Accessed November 8, 2011. http://www.saveur.com/article/Recipes/Eggs-Benedict.

"Eggs Hussarde Recipe." Brennan's Restaurant. Accessed November 8, 2011. http://www.brennansneworleans.com/r_eggshussarde.html.

Elliott, P. T. *100 Proof: Tips and Tales for Spirited Drinkers Everywhere*. New York: Plume, 2000.

Engel, Leo. *American & Other Drinks: Cocktails, Punches & Fancy Drinks*. London: Tinsley Brothers, 1878.

"English Cobbler." *CocktailDB*. Accessed September 21 2011. http://www.cocktaildb.com/recipe_detail?id=745.

"Escapist Refreshments." *Esquire*. January 1942.

Esquire, Inc. *The Art of Mixing Drinks: Based on Esquire Drink Book*. New York: Bantam, 1957.

Faith, William Robert. *Bob Hope: A Life in Comedy*. Cambridge: Da Capo, 2003.

Field, Colin Peter. *Cocktails of the Ritz Paris*. New York: Simon & Schuster, 2003.

Flirtini Cocktail—A Drink with Lime Twist. *Gourmet Cocktail*. Accessed March 3, 2012. http://cocktails.gourmetrecipe.com/cocktails-with-vodka-flirtini_l138.

"Full English Breakfast Quiche." *AllAboutYou.com*. Accessed November 4, 2011. http://www.allaboutyou.com/food/recipefinder/english-breakfast-quiche-recipe-51962.

Grimes, William. "At Brunch, the More Bizarre the Better." *New York Times*, July 8, 1998. Accessed September 12, 2011. http://www.nytimes.com/1998/07/08/dining/at-brunch-the-more-bizarre-the-better.html.

Guste, Roy R. "Antoine's Restaurant—New Orleans Cuisine, New Orleans Louisiana—Cafe Brulot." Accessed May 22, 2011. http://www.antoines.com/cafebrulot.html.

Haigh, Ted. *Vintage Spirits and Forgotten Cocktails*. Beverly, MA: Quarry Books, 2009.

Halley, Ned. *Wordsworth Dictionary of Drink*. Hertfordshire: Wordsworth Editions, 2005.

Handler, David. *The Boy Who Never Grew Up*. New York: Doubleday, 1992.

Hellmich, Mittie. *The Ultimate Bar Book*. San Francisco: Chronicle, 2006.

Herbst, Sharon Tyler, and Rob Herbst. *The Ultimate A-to-Z Bar Guide*. New York: Random House, 1998.

Hesser, Amanda. "1935: Ramos Gin Fizz." *New York Times*, June 15, 2008. Accessed September 12, 2011. http://www.nytimes.com/2008/06/15/magazine/15food-t-001.html.

"How to Make the BV Irish Coffee." The Buena Vista Café. Accessed May 22, 2011. http://www.thebuenavista.com/irishcoffee2.html.

"The Irish Coffee Story." The Buena Vista Café. Accessed May 22, 2011. http://www.thebuenavista.com/irishcoffee.html.

Kappeler, George J. *Modern American Drinks*. New York: Merriam, 1895.

Kingwell, Mark. *Classic Cocktails: A Modern Shake*. Toronto: McClelland & Stewart, 2006.

Kutch, Brenna. "How to Infuse Your Own Sweet Tea Vodka." *Portland Examiner*. Accessed August 9, 2011. http://www.examiner.com /couples-cooking-in-portland/how-to-infuse-your-own-sweet -tea-vodka.

Lendler, Ian. *Alcoholica Esoterica*. New York: Penguin, 2005.

Levine, Ed. "Sunday Brunch: Bourbon Vanilla French Toast." *Serious Eats*. Accessed November 5, 2011. http://www.seriouseats.com /recipes/2008/06/sunday_brunch_bourbon_vanilla_french _toast.html.

Meehan, Jim. *The PDT Cocktail Book: The Complete Bartender's Guide from the Celebrated Speakeasy*. New York: Sterling Epicure, 2011.

Newman, Kara. " 'Backs' Are Back." *Food Republic*. Accessed November 9, 2011. http://www.foodrepublic.com/2011/03/11/backs-are-back.

"Niçoise Tuna Sandwich (Pan Bagnat)." *Epicurious*. Accessed November 5, 2011. http://www.epicurious.com/recipes/food/views /Ni-oise-Tuna-Sandwich-Pan-Bagnat-104642.

O'Neil, Darcy. "Orgeat Syrup." *Art of Drink*. Accessed August 9, 2011. http://www.artofdrink.com/ingredients/syrups/orgeat-syrup.

Popik, Barry. "The Big Apple: Entry for Freddie Fudpucker or Freddy Fudpucker (Cocktail)." Accessed August 19, 2011. http://www.barrypopik.com/index.php/new_york_city/entry /freddie_fudpucker_cocktail.

Rea, Brian F. "*Old* Drink Book Reviews—1879 '*American & Other Drinks*,' by Leo Engel." *TheBarkeeper.com* 2, no. 2 (2010), 4.

"Recipe: White Sangria." *New York Times*. Accessed November 4, 2011. http://www.nytimes.com/2007/06/27/dining/271drex.html.

Richardson, Collette, ed. *House & Garden's Drink Guide: What Drinks to Serve When—And How to Make Them*. New York: Simon & Schuster, 1973.

Russock, Caroline. "Cook the Book: James Beard's Champagne Punch." *Serious Eats*. Accessed August 16, 2011. http:// www.seriouseats.com/recipes/2011/01/james-beards -champagne-punch-recipe.html.

Schmidt, William. *The Flowing Bowl: When and What to Drink*. New York: Charles L. Webster, 1892.

Sennett, Bob. *The Complete World Bartender Guide*. New York: Bantam Dell, 2007.

Shatkin, Elina. "The Pickled Pig: Eric Alperin Mixes Bacon and Gin." *Los Angeles Times*. Accessed July 3, 2011. http://latimesblogs .latimes.com/dailydish/2009/02/pickled-pig-bac.html.

Simmons, Krista. "Mixology Issue: Breakfast Cocktails Let You Have Your Drinks Over Easy." *Brand X*. Accessed June 18, 2011. http:// thisisbrandx.com/2011/02/breakfast-cocktails-having-your -drinks-over-easy.

Simmons, Marcia. "Maple Bacon Bloody Mary." Drink of the Week. Accessed November 1, 2011. http://www.drinkoftheweek.com /drink-of-the-week/maple-bacon-bloody-mary.

Simmons, Marcia, and Jonas Halpren. *DIY Cocktails: A Simple Guide to Creating Your Own Signature Drinks*. Avon, MA: Adams Media, 2011.

"Skier's Smoothie." *CocktailDB*. Accessed September 18, 2011. http:// www.cocktaildb.com/recipe_detail?id=2127.

Spunt, Alexandra. "10 Healthy Ways to Help a Hangover." *Good*. Accessed June 18, 2011. http://www.good.is/post/10-healthy-ways-to-help-a-hangover.

"Suffering Bastard." The Webtender Wiki. Accessed January 17, 2012. http://wiki.webtender.com/wiki/Suffering_Bastard.

"Tea 'Healthier' Drink than Water." *BBC News*. Accessed November 9, 2011. http://news.bbc.co.uk/2/hi/5281046.stm.

"Tea (Pepys' Diary)." *The Diary of Samuel Pepys*. Accessed November 9, 2011. http://www.pepysdiary.com/p/360.php#references.

Thomas, Jerry. *Bar-Tenders Guide*. New York: Dick & Fitzgerald, 1887.

Thompson, Al. "Bloody Mary Inventor Likes Sipping Scotch." *Cleveland Press*, January 1, 1972.

"Vodka Espresso aka Pharmaceutical Stimulant aka Espresso Martini." Casa Coctel. Accessed August 22, 2011. http://www.casacoctel.com/index.php?option=com_rapidrecipe&page=viewrecipe&recipe_id=120.

Walton, Stuart. *The Ultimate Book of Cocktails*. East Bridgewater, MA: World Publications Group, 2007.

"Watermelon Feta & Red Onion Salad." *SparkRecipes*. Accessed November 7, 2011. http://recipes.sparkpeople.com/recipe-detail.asp?recipe=133946.

Williams, Gregory Paul. *The Story of Hollywood*. Los Angeles: BL Press, 2005.

Wondrich, David. "How to Make the Perfect Black Velvet." *Esquire*. Accessed August 12, 2011. http://www.esquire.com/drinks/black-velvet-drink-recipe.

———. "How to Make the Perfect Cafe Cocktail." *Esquire*. Accessed June 18, 2011. http://www.esquire.com/drinks/cafe-cocktail-drink-recipe.

———. "How to Make the Perfect Cafe Grog." *Esquire*. Accessed June 18, 2011. http://www.esquire.com/drinks/cafe-grog-drink-recipe.

———. "How to Make the Perfect Champagne Punch." *Esquire*. Accessed August 16, 2011. http://www.esquire.com/drinks/champagne-punch-drink-recipe.

———. "How to Make the Perfect Irish Coffee." *Esquire*. Accessed May 22, 2011. http://www.esquire.com/drinks/irish-coffee-drink-recipe.

———. "How to Make the Perfect Ramos Fizz." *Esquire*. Accessed September 13, 2011. http://www.esquire.com/drinks/ramos-fizz-drink-recipe.

———. *Imbibe!: From Absinthe Cocktail to Whiskey Smash, a Salute in Stories and Drinks to "Professor" Jerry Thomas, Pioneer of the American Bar*. New York: Perigee, 2007.

Young, Daniel. *Coffee Love: 50 Ways to Drink Your Java*. New York: Wiley, 2009.

index

about the author and the photographer

Peter Joseph has written about cocktails and pop culture for *Flavorwire*, *Lost Magazine*, and *Popmatters*. In between brunches, he is an editor at Thomas Dunne Books. He lives in Brooklyn, New York. Learn more at www.peterjoseph.us.

Salma Khalil was born in Alexandria, Egypt, and received her MFA in photography at the Pratt Institute in New York. She has shown her work around the United States, including at the Center for Fine Art Photography in Colorado, Woman Made Gallery in Chicago, Studio Gallery in Washington, DC, and Umbrella Arts and PS122 Gallery in New York City. Learn more at www.salmatkhalil.com.